WITHDRAWAL

Achieving Excellence

in School Counseling

Through Motivation, Self-Direction,
Self-Knowledge and Relationships

This book is dedicated to

Clarence (Curly) Johnson, Sharon Johnson
and Ron Frederickson

Drs. Clarence (Curly) Johnson's and Sharon Johnson's seminal work
on results-based school counseling brought clarity of purpose and potential
to our thinking. They taught us how to stay focused on results
that make a difference in students' lives, and to grasp the full power and
potential of delivering learner-centered school counseling programs.

Dr. Ronald Fredrickson taught us the importance of research-based
school counseling practice. His focus on basing decisions about
school counseling practice on the best available empirical evidence
inspired the creation of the Center for School Counseling Outcome
Research & Evaluation (CSCORE), and continues to motivate all our
efforts to promote the adoption of evidence-based school counseling.

Karl L. Squier   Patricia Nailor   John C. Carey

Foreword by Clarence and Sharon Johnson

Achieving Excellence

in School Counseling

Through Motivation, Self-Direction,
Self-Knowledge and Relationships

CORWIN
A SAGE Company

HARVARD UNIVERSITY
GRADUATE SCHOOL OF EDUCATION
MONROE C. GUTMAN LIBRARY

CORWIN
A SAGE Company

FOR INFORMATION:

Corwin
A SAGE Company
2455 Teller Road
Thousand Oaks, California 91320
(800) 233-9936
www.corwin.com

SAGE Publications Ltd.
1 Oliver's Yard
55 City Road
London EC1Y 1SP
United Kingdom

SAGE Publications India Pvt. Ltd.
B 1/I 1 Mohan Cooperative Industrial Area
Mathura Road, New Delhi 110 044
India

SAGE Publications Asia-Pacific Pte. Ltd.
3 Church Street
#10-04 Samsung Hub
Singapore 049483

Acquisitions Editor: Jessica Allan
Associate Editor: Kimberly Greenberg
Editorial Assistant: Cesar Reyes
Project Editor: Libby Larson
Copy Editor: Terri Lee Paulsen
Typesetter: C&M Digitals (P) Ltd.
Proofreader: Rae-Ann Godwin
Indexer: Maria Sosnowski
Cover Designer: Michael Dubowe
Marketing Manager: Stephanie Trkay

Copyright © 2014 by Corwin

Printed in the United States of America.

Library of Congress Cataloging-in-Publication Data

Squier, Karl L.

Achieving excellence in school counseling through motivation, self-direction, self-knowledge, and relationships / Karl L. Squier, Patricia Nailor, John C. Carey.

pages cm.
Includes bibliographical references and index.

ISBN 978-1-4833-0672-8 (pbk. : alk. paper)

1. Educational counseling—United States. 2. Motivation in education—United States. 3. Academic achievement—United States. I. Title.

LB1027.5.S66 2014
371.4'220973—dc23   2014009340

SFI   Certified Sourcing
      www.sfiprogram.org
      SFI-00453

14 15 16 17 18 10 9 8 7 6 5 4 3 2 1

Contents

List of Figures

Foreword

It is a pleasure to write the Foreword for this valuable resource book on a construct-based approach to school counseling. It promises to provide the means to unite the important achievements of results-based school counseling programs, systems planning, and the benefits of evidence-based research. The authors are noted professionals who have worked for many years in the field of school counseling and have been recognized leaders locally, statewide, nationally, and internationally. The development of this book has benefitted from their understanding of the history of school counseling and its future potential.

Dr. Karl Squier is well-known for his work in systems design, planning, curriculum development, and a toolkit approach to implementing comprehensive school counseling programs. Dr. Patricia Nailor's extensive experience as a school counselor, school administrator, counselor educator, and past president of the American School Counselor Association provides a broad base of knowledge and skills required by a results-based school counseling program. Dr. John Carey has extensive experience in school counseling and evidence-based practices research. As Director of the Ronald H. Fredrickson Center for School Counseling Outcome Research & Evaluation (CSCORE) at the University of Massachusetts, Amherst, he has been a leading advocate for ensuring that the school counseling profession is thoroughly grounded in research and evidence-based practice. The combination of their three unique perspectives brings a new view and a powerful influence in school counselors' efforts to ensure student success.

The profession of school counseling has experienced numerous iterations from its beginnings as a service provider to the current focus of building comprehensive school counseling programs geared to achieving student results. The journey has been a curved and winding road, but counseling programs have emerged as a valuable element within effective education programs. Counselors have become active partners in achieving the mission of districts, schools, parents, and communities.

Traditionally, counselors were held accountable for a list of duties identified in a job description. These expectations evolved from defined processes (what each counselor was to do) to identification of how students would be different as the result of the counseling program. It was a fundamental shift from services to results-based programs. Some believed that it was impossible to define the results of counseling programs, therefore only the processes were assessed, with the expectation that if the counselors adhered to specific processes, the students would benefit. The more fundamental question, however, is: How are students different as the result of the counselors' efforts and through participation in the school counseling program?

The mission of school counseling is to ensure that all students are successful. The importance of student results in this endeavor cannot be ignored. Now is the time to question our assumptions and move toward student results as the central focus of school counseling. Although many different models are available, multiple curriculum activities implemented, and data collected using evidence-based strategies, without a clear target they are arrows aimed in a direction that may or may not connect with all students. Results-based programs are proactively designed, based on research-validated models that are consistent with expected developmental stages of learning.

Results-based programs are assessed on student success and in the end, it is only the student's achievement that is relevant to the effectiveness of a counseling program or any other education program. Assessment of progress is individual, and group strategies to collect data to determine success are often just data-based programs vs. student-based programs. Success for one student is not necessarily the same for others. Implementation and assessment must use clearly stated, predetermined student results as the focus for the program. Agreement on results provides the unifying basis for wider collaboration within the educational community and for wider collaboration with families and communities. Results data demonstrate competence in identified, specific knowledge, attitudes, or skills. The purpose of evaluation is to improve the program.

We cannot speak to student results without acknowledging the pioneers of this concept, including the results-based systems of Dr. Roger Kaufman, the early statewide trials in Arizona under the direction of Dr. Tina Ammons, the support of the professional organizations including ASCA and ACA, as well as collaboration with Dr. Anita Mitchell with American Institutes of Research and Dr. Martin Gerstein of Virginia Tech.

This book is a vital next step for the school counseling profession by defining what results we expect students to achieve based on research. Not only do the authors propose standards for student excellence, but also how to deliver meaningful learning opportunities and assess student progress toward, and achievement of, the standards. This generation is faced with social change to a degree that has never before been seen or even imagined. In many cases the students are beyond the educators in their knowledge and skills in technology and other fields, but they have little idea of their role or sense of their possible selves in the future.

The value of this book is that it provides an avenue for counselors, teachers, administrators, students, families, and communities to work together to ensure student achievement and future success. By uniting the results-based approach to achieving student excellence with a systemic plan for implementation and assessment, the school counseling program will allow all the responsible adults in a student's life to work together to guarantee success.

Clarence Johnson, Ph.D., Retired

Sharon Johnson, Ed.D., Professor Emeritus

Acknowledgments

The work that is documented in this publication emerged from years of dialogue and reflection between and among many professional colleagues. We gratefully acknowledge the stimulating discussions we have had over the years with so many of our colleagues.

We wish to thank the members of a former ASCA committee who contributed to the discussion of standards and constructs: Jim Bierma, Jill Cook, Carol Dahir, Julie Hartline, Donna Hoffman, Tammi Mackaben, Shirley Pate, Eric Sparks and Richard Wong.

We would like to thank our close colleagues and friends who have contributed to the Construct-Based Approach through both their support and challenges. These special colleagues include Karen Harrington, Katie Gray, Ian Martin, Brett Zyromski, Gina Franco, Jason Schweid, Jean Greco, Carey Dimmitt, Belinda Wilkerson, Pat Martin and Carlos Turriago.

To all the school counselors who have been working to support their students with their school counseling program, you inspire us and motivate us to do this work. Thank you; we hope this book will help you make a difference in your students' lives.

Finally, we wish to thank all the wonderful people at Corwin who have made this a productive and manageable process. Their dedication and pursuit of excellence throughout the production process has been exemplary. We wish to thank those at Corwin with whom we have interacted most closely: Libby Larson for her guidance as project editor, Terri Lee Paulsen for her thoroughness and editing skills as our copy editor, and Cesar Reyes for his ongoing assistance in resolving issues and meeting deadlines. A special thanks to Jessica Allan, acquisitions editor, who recognized the transformative potential of a construct-based approach (CBA) to school counseling, and has been so supportive from the very beginning.

PUBLISHER'S ACKNOWLEDGMENTS

Corwin gratefully acknowledges the contributions of the following reviewers:

Stuart Chen-Hayes, Ph.D.
Associate Professor & Program Coordinator, Counselor Education/School Counseling
Lehman College of the City University of New York
Bronx, New York

Gloria Avolio DePaul, Ph.D.
School Counselor
School District of Hillsborough County
Tampa, Florida

Jon M. Shepard
School Psychologist
Denton Independent School District
Denton, Texas

About the Authors

Dr. Karl L. Squier has been a consultant to education and business for more than 35 years and has been working in the field of professional school counseling for 15 years. Karl has consulted with local school districts, state school counselor associations, state departments of education, and national school counseling organizations and initiatives.

Dr. Squier has developed systemic reform initiatives for school districts and has created a toolkits approach to implementing school counseling programs for all students. He advocates for the school counseling curriculum as a primary vehicle for helping students achieve excellence. Karl is a children's book author and creator of integrated learning systems for all levels along the K–12 learning continuum.

Dr. Patricia Nailor is a former school counselor and supervisor of school counselors. Now retired, Dr. Nailor is an adjunct instructor at Providence College, Providence, Rhode Island, in the Graduate Program in Counselor Education. Additionally, she consults with school districts in the development and implementation of school counseling programs.

Dr. Nailor has served as president and professional development chair of the Rhode Island School Counselor Association (RISCA). She served on the American School Counselor Association's (ASCA) Governing Board as the vice president of the North Atlantic Region and as ASCA's president in 2009–2010.

Dr. John C. Carey is a Professor of School Counseling and the Director of the Ronald H. Fredrickson Center for School Counseling Outcome Research & Evaluation (CSCORE) at the University of Massachusetts, Amherst. Dr. Carey is a national leader in the evidence-based school counseling movement and has coauthored the influential book *Evidence-Based School Counseling: Making a Difference With Data-Driven Practices* with Corwin.

Dr. Carey is currently involved in the development and evaluation of research-based interventions in schools. He is the co-principal investigator of an Institute of Education Sciences–funded efficacy study of *Student Success Skills*. He is also collaborating in the development and evaluation of *Eccomi Pronto,* a school counseling curriculum designed to facilitate the development of self-direction skills in young students in Italian primary schools.

Dr. Carey has coauthored numerous research articles including recent statewide evaluations of the effectiveness of school counseling programs in Utah and Nebraska, and a national study of the level of implementation of state school counseling models. He is a frequent conference presenter at the major school counseling conferences.

Dr. Carey is also active in the globalization of school counseling. He assisted the University of Verona to design and implement the first master's program in school counseling in Italy. In addition, he was recently named to the Fulbright Specialist Roster and, through this vehicle, will be helping other international universities improve their school counselor education programs by embracing evidence-based practice.

1 Introduction

Scenario 1

Sonia was delighted to be hired by Elm School District as its first elementary school counselor. Fresh from her graduate program, she was excited to implement all she had learned about comprehensive school counseling programs. She arrived at her school on Orientation Day to find she had no office or supplies, and no one, including her principal, knew why she was there. She spent the entire first quarter of the school year building relationships with faculty and staff and offering to hold groups for children on topics she gleaned from conversations with her colleagues.

By December, she felt she was making some headway to being accepted in her school by adults, and the students with whom she had interacted loved her and greeted her enthusiastically in the halls and cafeteria. However, she felt overwhelmed facing an uphill battle to gain access to students, fielding continually increasing noncounseling duties assigned by her principal and still having to "build" a program. She felt her principal was not listening, or did not believe anything Sonia said about the need for children to have the benefit of a school counseling curriculum. Sonia did not know how to get started and hoped her second year would be better.

Scenario 2

Sonia came to the Elm School District to be the first elementary counselor in the district fresh from her graduate program with an understanding of a research-backed, educational construct-based school counseling program. She approached her principal, Dr. Smith, with a folder she had prepared that included construct-based student standards, the research behind them and a plan for how she would implement her program in each grade. Dr. Smith was impressed by Sonia's enthusiasm about making a difference for all the children in the elementary school and the research behind her approach. Although unsure of the need for such a program, the principal gave Sonia a chance to prove herself. She introduced her to the faculty and staff with the directive to give her access to students for full class and small group instruction.

Sonia spent the first quarter building relationships with her colleagues and helping them sort through some of the issues students were presenting by offering classroom or small group instruction on those topics. By the end of the second quarter, she had gained the trust of many teachers who offered her access to their students for classroom lessons. At the end of the school year, Sonia made a PowerPoint presentation to her principal and faculty demonstrating with data the impact she had made that year with students. Sonia's program was deemed a success, and she spent the next few years building a complete program and gaining the trust of even the most recalcitrant teachers.

Reflections

Having research to describe the potential of constructs on students' learning is a powerful tool counselors can use to convince administrators that the school counseling program deserves a chance. Backing the argument up with data demonstrating the positive impact on students should seal the deal. Sometimes enthusiasm and knowledge just aren't enough.

PURPOSE OF BOOK

Research provides data that can be used in decision-making processes related to school counseling programs and school counselor practice. It helps determine what works and does not work and suggests the ramifications of pursuing one path over another. The purpose of this book is to articulate a Construct-Based Approach (CBA) to school counseling that encompasses rigorous school counseling student standards, challenging learning opportunities delivered through a standards-based curriculum, and assessments that help determine student proficiency and achievement in relation to the counseling standards.

The CBA is anchored in more than 50 years of research related to student learning and development. Research was reviewed to identify educational constructs within the purview of school counseling that have the greatest potential for school counselors impacting student lives in positive ways.

The book began as a dialog about school counseling student standards and what research findings from education and the social sciences would identify as critical areas of student growth and development that could be effectively addressed by school counseling programs. This evolved into a closer examination of the processes involved in establishing research-based student standards. From this exploration emerged two powerful perspectives that can significantly impact the way school counseling programs are designed, delivered and evaluated: "construct-based" and "results-based."

Construct-Based Perspective

Educational constructs focus on various aspects of human thinking and behavior that are critical to student development, achievement and success. Although there are many constructs that could be used, four have been selected for the foundation of a construct-based approach to school counseling: a) motivation, b) self-direction, c) self-knowledge and d) relationships.

These have been selected because researchers have demonstrated that they are critical areas in student development in which school counselors can have a significant impact and because they are strongly linked to learning and achievement. Focusing on these four constructs potentially enables school counselors to more fully support students' academic achievement, guide their preparation for future success through educational and career planning, and help them cope with barriers to their learning.

Results-Based Perspective

A results-based perspective clearly defines what students are expected to know and demonstrate as a consequence of the school counseling program. There are two primary types of student results: standards and competencies. Standard statements define what students should know and do by the time they graduate from high school. In addition, students are expected to demonstrate proficiency in achieving developmentally appropriate competencies along the K–12 learning continuum. Student progress toward and achievement of the competencies and standards are monitored and assessed. School counseling is a results-based program because its primary focus is on achieving results that make a difference in student lives.

A challenging curriculum is developed based on the constructs and results students are expected to achieve. A results-based approach contains core curriculum activities to be delivered to all students. Core curriculum provides three types of opportunities: a) opportunities to learn what is being taught, b) opportunities to apply what they are learning in authentic contexts and c) opportunities to demonstrate what they know and can do as a result of their learning. The school counseling curriculum is the primary vehicle for delivering a standards-based program wherein all students strive to achieve the same standards of excellence and can be uniformly assessed in terms of their progress toward the standards.

Book + Tools

This book (*Achieving Excellence in School Counseling through Motivation, Self-Direction, Self-Knowledge and Relationships*) provides the research base and conceptual foundation for a CBA. The *CBA Toolkit* (hereafter Toolkit) provides a set of simple tools to help you design, deliver and evaluate your CBA program.

The role of school counselors is to help students develop the knowledge, skills, attitudes, beliefs and habits of mind that enable them to profit maximally from their instructional opportunities and experiences. This book uses well-researched constructs that have been demonstrated to play a significant role in student growth and development.

The premise of this book is that by focusing primarily on these four constructs to build a construct-based approach to school counseling programs, students will become better learners and higher achievers. This can be accomplished through school counselors helping students think about how they think, learn about how they learn, and consider how their thinking and behavior patterns influence and have consequences in their lives.

This effort to reframe the discussion about school counseling student standards and how to help students achieve meaningful results is a journey of exploration into possibility and potential. We invite you to share this journey with us.

HOW BOOK CHAPTERS ARE ORGANIZED

Each chapter consists of three parts. Part 1 begins with two scenarios that help establish actual situations in which the chapter content would be relevant. Part 2 contains the body of the chapter. Part 3 is a "Construction Zone," which delineates what you can expect to learn and do by using the Toolkit tools associated with each chapter.

BOOK CHAPTER DESCRIPTIONS

Chapter 1 ("Introduction") describes the book's purpose and provides an overview of chapters and of the *CBA Toolkit,* a set of tools for designing, delivering and evaluating CBA programs.

Chapter 2 ("A Simple Language Set") provides key terminology and a conceptual framework for discussing the role of research-based constructs in establishing school counseling student standards and competencies in K–12 school counseling programs. A simple language set for discussing construct, results and standards-based school counseling program is offered.

Chapter 3 ("Research-Based Constructs") reviews the research regarding educational and social science constructs that are highly relevant to the school counselor's role. Four constructs have been selected as the foundation of a CBA: motivation, self-direction, self-knowledge and relationships. Although there are other constructs or terms that could be used, it was concluded that these four represented the most significant potential for helping school counselors respond to students' needs.

Chapter 4 ("Relevant Contexts for K–12 School Counseling Programs") discusses the importance of "context" in developing standard and competency statements. Core contexts addressed include academic support, student planning (individual learning plans), college and career readiness, personal growth, and social interaction.

Chapter 5 ("Student Results: Standards and Competencies") provides potential standard and competency statements for a CBA. Twelve standard statements are proposed, three statements for each of the four constructs. Sample competency statements aligned with the standards are also provided.

Chapter 6 ("Role of Curriculum in a CBA") focuses on a rigorous school counseling curriculum that supports students becoming highly motivated and self-directed learners, who know about themselves and are engaged in meaningful relationships. Developing and delivering quality learning opportunities that enable students to achieve the standards are discussed.

Chapter 7 ("Assessing Student Proficiency and Achievement in a CBA") describes the essential components of the student assessment process and how to determine student progress toward, and achievement of, the CBA student standards. Assessments embedded in curriculum activities and at end of level are described, and sample assessment instruments are provided. Suggestions on how to report data on student progress on report cards are also included.

Chapter 8 ("CBA Program Implementation: Focus on Planning") describes a complete planning cycle for school counseling that includes goal setting and action planning. Four types of plans essential to a CBA are strategic plans, annual implementation plans, counselor-supervisor agreements and school counselors' personal plans for achieving results during the school year.

Chapter 9 ("CBA Program Implementation: Focus on Delivery") examines some key operation requirements for establishing an effective support system for the successful delivery of a CBA program: roles and accountabilities, policies and protocols, fluid communication, data management and professional development.

Chapter 10 ("CBA Program Implementation: Focus on Evaluation") discusses central concepts in evaluating the efficacy and impact of a CBA on student achievement and school improvement.

Chapter 11 ("CBA's Contribution to School Improvement Initiatives") explores ways in which a CBA can a) contribute to national school counseling efforts (ASCA National Model, evidence-based school counseling practice), b) support the implementation of national initiatives for redefining knowledge and skill requirements (Common Core, Partnership for 21st Century Skills) and c) find significant common ground with school-based intervention systems (Response to Intervention, Positive Behavioral Interventions and Supports, and Early-Warning Systems).

Chapter 12 ("Power and Potential") describes the promise and benefits of a CBA to the future of school counseling and education reform.

FROM CONCEPT TO PRACTICE

The CBA has both a conceptual foundation, which is presented in this book, and a set of tools (*CBA Toolkit*) for implementing a CBA. In order to provide the concepts and point to relevant tools, the chapters in the book are all organized in three main sections. Two scenarios begin the chapter to help contextualize the chapter's content. These are followed by the main body of the chapter, which provides the conceptual underpinnings for a CBA. The third section is a Construction Zone at the end of each chapter that specifies what you can expect to learn and do by using the *CBA Toolkit*. Figure 1.1 shows what is provided in the book and the *CBA Toolkit*.

CBA TOOLKIT COMPONENTS

The *CBA Toolkit* helps school counselors design and implement a construct-based approach in their K–12 school counseling programs. It assists counselors in setting rigorous standards for student excellence, delivering and managing the CBA program, and evaluating its impact on student achievement and school improvement.

Figure 1.1 From Concept to Practice

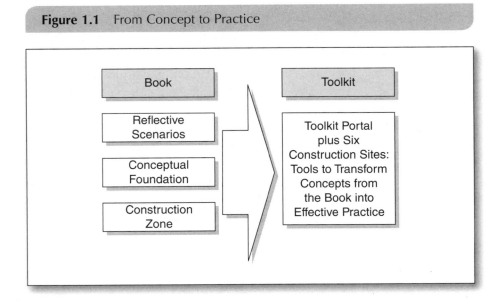

The *CBA Toolkit* is a companion to *Achieving Excellence in School Counseling through Motivation, Self-Direction, Self-Knowledge and Relationships*. The book provides a conceptual framework for the CBA that is grounded in research and demonstrates the power and potential of a CBA to school counseling programs. Whereas the book focuses on the conceptual framing of a CBA (student standards, curriculum, student assessments), the Toolkit focuses on the operational requirements for establishing and sustaining a CBA (program design, delivery and evaluation). Figure 1.2 displays the *CBA Toolkit* Portal and six Construction Sites.

Learner-Centered Construction Sites focus on building the content of a CBA program (knowledge and skill requirements, curriculum, assessments). The Program Implementation Construction Sites focus on designing, planning, implementing and evaluating the program.

The *CBA Toolkit* is a set of planning, delivery and evaluation tools capable of establishing sustainable processes (e.g., strategic, annual and personal planning processes) and producing products (e.g., Curriculum Framework for School Counseling describing the programmatic approach to supporting students). Likewise, it is recommended that an operational guide be produced (Administrative Handbook for School Counseling) that describes critical areas that must be addressed to successfully implement a CBA school counseling program.

Figure 1.2 *CBA Toolkit* Portal

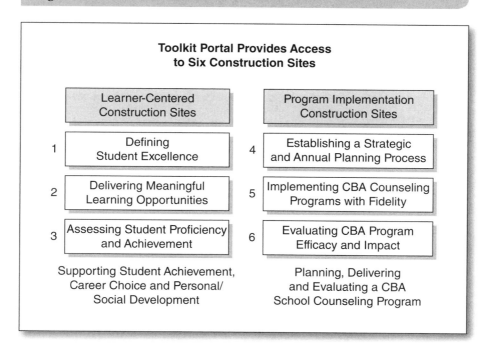

The *CBA Toolkit* can help school counselors introduce a CBA program in their schools and/or districts by helping them define student excellence, develop a challenging curriculum and assess student progress toward the school counseling student standards. The *CBA Toolkit* is a comprehensive implementation plan for districts wanting to implement a construct-based approach to school counseling. The CBA has great potential for helping students with their metacognitive skill development, learning how to reflect on their learning experiences and improving their thinking and behavioral processes.

CONSTRUCTION SITE COMPONENTS

The *CBA Toolkit* consists of seven work sites (a Portal and six Construction Sites). These sites are the building blocks of a CBA. All seven sites are organized in the same way (see Figure 1.3).

Figure 1.3 Construction Site Contents

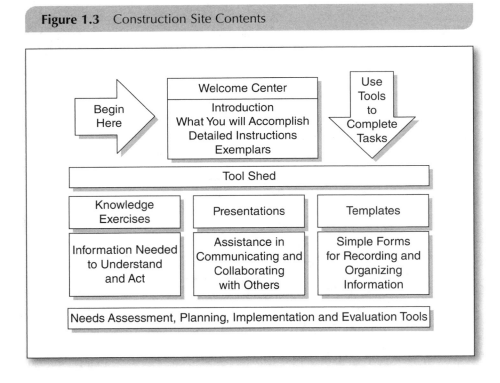

The Toolkit provides the tools to implement the CBA program described in this book. The following chart shows which construction sites (CS) are used with each chapter.

Chapter	Chapter Title	Sites
1	"Introduction"	Portal
2	"A Simple Language Set"	Portal
3	"Research-Based Constructs"	CS1
4	"Relevant Contexts for K–12 School Counseling Programs"	CS1
5	"Student Results: Standards and Competencies"	CS1
6	"Role of Curriculum in a CBA"	CS2
7	"Assessing Student Proficiency and Achievement in a CBA"	CS3
8	"CBA Program Implementation: Focus on Planning"	CS4
9	"CBA Program Implementation: Focus on Delivery"	CS5
10	"CBA Program Implementation: Focus on Evaluation"	CS6
11	"CBA's Contribution to School Improvement Initiatives"	CS4
12	"Power and Potential"	N/A

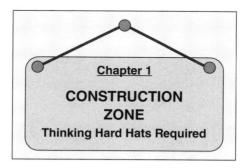

The tools located in the Portal section of the *CBA Toolkit* can be used in conjunction with Chapter 1. Some readers may wish to read the entire book first before starting on the Toolkit. Others may prefer to begin exploring the Toolkit from the very beginning. In that case, go to the *CBA Toolkit,* enter the Portal and follow the instructions provided at the Portal Welcome Center.

The Navigation Guide provides instructions for considering and promoting the key terms that define a CBA. Two presentations provide an overview of the Toolkit and a summary of the foundational principles of a CBA school counseling program.

The *CBA Toolkit* consists of seven work sites (a Portal and six Construction Sites). Access to the tools is through the Toolkit Portal, where you will learn about the purpose of the Toolkit, how it is organized and the results you can expect to accomplish by using the tools. All sites contain three types of tools:

- Knowledge exercises, which provide information you will need to understand and successfully complete critical tasks.

- Presentations to present a high-level overview of each site's main focus and which can be used to communicate with others regarding a CBA.

- Templates that are broadly defined as tools requiring data and/or decision making (e.g., data input templates, checklists).

The intent of the *CBA Toolkit* is to help you develop a construct-based approach to school counseling for your district and integrate it into your counseling program. At the Toolkit Portal Welcome Center you will receive a Navigation Guide that shows how easy it is to navigate among all the sites and individual tools. The guide contains an annotated index of all tools in the Toolkit along with a brief description of each tool and the filenames of all the files.

CONNECTING CHAPTER 1 TO THE TOOLKIT PORTAL

What you can expect to learn and do:

- ✓ Conduct a needs assessment on the readiness of your school counseling program to implement a CBA.

- ✓ Understand the purpose of the *CBA Toolkit* and how it is organized.

- ✓ Describe how a CBA can increase the capacity of school counselors to make a difference in student lives.

- ✓ Describe the benefits of developing and integrating a CBA in your school counseling program.

- ✓ Develop an initial plan for completing all Toolkit activities.

Looking forward to working with you at the CBA Toolkit Portal!

2 A Simple Language Set

Scenario 1

The Policy and Governance Committee of the State School Counselor Association met for a planning session to write a white paper to support the development of a school counselor–specific evaluation tool in the new evaluation process being considered by the State Board of Education. The Committee was comprised of school counselors from several districts who represented all levels of education. As the meeting progressed, it became apparent that the counselors did not have the same understanding of terms. Some referred to "standards" that others called "competencies," while someone else questioned whether a "competency" was actually an "indicator," and no one was sure if they should refer to "benchmarks" since they had no clear understanding of how they are measured. Setting aside the conversation on terms, the committee decided to just describe a comprehensive school counseling program in their paper. Again, the members were not in sync about the elements of a program. The frustrated Chair of the Committee decided to adjourn the meeting and reschedule.

Scenario 2

At a board meeting of the State School Counselor Association, a discussion ensued about whether, in light of impending new policy on counselor evaluation, the Board should issue a white paper regarding the role of the school counselor in student achievement and how the school counseling program is a "value added" component of a successful education. Many of the Board members had a clear understanding of the Construct-Based Approach (CBA) to school counseling and argued that since research backed the approach, it would be in the best interest of all counselors in the state if the Association took a proactive stance. They decided to inform the State Board of Education and future evaluators of the potential positive impact on student learning when a construct-based program is in place. The Board formed a committee to write a paper. At the committee's first meeting, the Chair asked each member of his/her understanding of the language set, and they reached a consensus on terms and set about assigning tasks to get the job done.

Reflections

The construct-based approach to developing a school counseling program offers a clear set of terms that can help school counselors speak a common language and move the profession forward.

IMPORTANCE OF THE LANGUAGE WE USE

Discussions about student learning can be complex. It is never good to assume that everyone is on the same page when it comes to terminology and definitions, especially in discussions that are attempting to reframe the way we look at school counseling and how to improve it. This book is a reframing of how counselors look at student outcomes, curriculum delivery and student assessments based on research that suggests on which areas school counselors should focus to maximize their potential to positively impact student lives.

This chapter provides a simple language set that can be used to describe and discuss a Construct-Based Approach (CBA) to school counseling. These key terms define the core ideas used to build, deliver and evaluate a CBA program. Concise definitions will be useful with words like "standard," which have a long history in educational reform and multiple definitions. For a dialog on school counseling student standards, curriculum and assessments to produce meaningful results, the team members responsible for decisions and actions need to agree on the core terminology and definitions being used in the discussion.

Any language set will, over time, expand in the number of terms and the complexity of definitions and interconnections, but it is always important to be able to identify a core set of terms that can be consistently used to frame and advance the dialog. The following terms are considered to be central to a discussion about a CBA.

CONSTRUCT

Educational constructs focus on various aspects of human behavior that are critical to students' ability to think, learn, plan for their futures, make informed decisions about and be prepared to successfully pursue post-secondary opportunities.

Four research-based educational constructs have been selected to represent critical aspects of student learning on which school counselors can have the greatest impact: a) motivation, b) self-direction, c) self-knowledge and

d) relationships. Focusing on these constructs helps enable school counselors to support students' academic achievement, guide their preparation for future success through educational and career planning, and help them cope with the myriad challenges of learning and growing up.

The approach delineated in this book is called a "construct-based approach" (CBA) because these four constructs are the primary filters through which we understand and address student needs, and on which a CBA program can be built.

CONTEXT

The notion of "context" is used to describe a set of student-related processes or conditions that school counselors have a responsibility to address. There are many contexts that can be identified that are relevant to student development along the K–12 learning continuum, and which fall within the purview of school counselors' roles and accountabilities.

Five contexts have been selected for this discussion as they are critical to school counselors maximizing their potential in terms of a) student planning, b) academic support, c) college and career readiness, d) personal growth and e) social interaction. Each context contains processes, some of which are essential to students' ability to effectively respond to the demands of the context. Essential processes for each context are provided in Chapter 4 ("Relevant Contexts for K–12 School Counseling Programs").

RESULTS

The central focus of a CBA is on student results—what students are expected to know and demonstrate as a result of the school counseling program. Results establish clear expectations (outcomes) for student achievement and success. Results are the difference school counselors seek to make in student lives and learning.

From a programmatic perspective, results are the planned, measureable outcomes of an effective school counseling program. From a student perspective, results are the knowledge, attitudes and skills acquired and demonstrated by students because of their participation in the school counseling program.

Results are measurable in terms of processes students learn (e.g., relationship-building techniques, problem-solving methodology, conflict-resolution strategies) and products they produce (e.g., portfolio artifacts, career plans). Students are expected to do something that demonstrates how well they can apply what they have learned to authentic situations (proficiency).

The phrase "results-based" is used to indicate that results—the difference the counseling program and school counselors make in students' lives—are the primary focus of the school counseling profession (Johnson, Johnson, & Downs, 2006). There are two primary types of results for students—standards and competencies—that are used to define student excellence.

Standards

A standard is an end result to be achieved within a specified time frame. School counseling student standards are end results that students are expected to achieve by the time they graduate from high school. Use of the term "standard" is restricted to what students should know and be able to do by the end of Grade 12. It is not used to articulate what students should know and do along the K–12 learning continuum.

Competency

Student standards are articulated as statements that focus attention on key areas of student development. These statements, in and of themselves, however, are not measurable. For a standard to become measurable it must be contextualized, linked to authentic situations where it means something to counselors and students, and is relevant to success in the postsecondary world.

Competencies clarify the intent of the standard in measurable terms. According to Johnson et al. (2006), competencies are statements that describe requirements or conditions that must be met for a student to be deemed "proficient." They provide more precise examples of evidence and proficiency that can be used to determine student progress along the K–12 learning continuum.

Competencies are learned proficiencies that can be observed, transferred from a learning situation to a real-life situation and are related to the results the counseling program expects students to achieve. School counselors, students and parents use competencies to gauge the extent to which students are moving toward school counseling student standards.

Competencies can be organized in intervals (e.g., by level, grade) and can be distributed along a learning continuum. For example, a standard (end result) can have multiple competencies that require a demonstration of proficiency by the end of a specific time frame (e.g., middle school) or the end of a specific grade span (e.g., Grades 3–5) or the end of a specific learning activity (e.g., college and career exploration). Since competencies provide the level of specificity that is measurable, they must be developmentally appropriate and spiral across the K–12 learning continuum. Collectively, mastery of the competencies throughout the learning continuum enables students to achieve the student standards (end results for the school counseling program).

Student standards and competencies are important because they define the results students are expected to achieve across and by the end of the K–12 learning continuum. All standard and competency statements are contextualized in terms of human experience. Working toward standards requires students to not only acquire knowledge and develop skills, but to become proficient in applying them in real-life contexts. This requires students to demonstrate their proficiency in measurable ways and provides counselors with a way to determine student needs and progress toward the standards, and adjust their personal learning plans accordingly.

The ability to clearly define concrete results that are observable and measurable is critical to the successful implementation of comprehensive school counseling programs. Standards establish the long-range targets, while competencies define what students are expected to know and do along the learning continuum. A list of standard and competency statements on its own cannot ensure the successful implementation of a comprehensive school counseling program. These statements require a rigorous and documented counseling curriculum in addition to a wide range of counseling, family and community interventions.

CURRICULUM

Thus far, the key terms identified for a CBA (constructs, context, student results) all focus on defining student excellence. What is now needed is a standards-based delivery system that provides students with meaningful opportunities to achieve the expected results.

The primary vehicle in a CBA for using the student standards is the counseling curriculum. The curriculum is the only place in the school counseling program where all students can receive equal opportunities for learning and where their progress can be uniformly assessed.

Core curriculum activities that focus on motivation, self-direction, self-knowledge and relationships can be delivered that target those areas that research shows can potentially have a substantive impact on student achievement and success. The term "core" is used to identify those activities that are to be delivered to all students because of the importance of the content. All core counseling curriculum activities should be documented and contain embedded assessments for measuring student progress toward the expected results for the activity. Immediate feedback to students can then be ensured.

The core counseling curriculum consists of planned interventions (as opposed to responsive services, which are on-demand). Curriculum activities are planned learning experiences in which students and counselors interact to achieve specific results (learning outcomes). They are organized in a scope and sequence (delivery schedule). Curriculum activities contain clearly defined results—results students are expected to achieve. The core curriculum is an integrated set of activities that engages students and personalizes their learning experiences.

The school counseling curriculum is aligned with the CBA school counseling student standards and competencies. A rigorous (challenging) curriculum ensures that students are provided three types of opportunities: a) opportunities to Learn what they are being taught, b) opportunities to Apply what they have learned in authentic situations and c) opportunities to Demonstrate their proficiency in applying what they have learned. The counseling curriculum requires clearly articulated standards and competencies that define what students are expected to achieve (know and successfully demonstrate). They are based on knowledge and skill requirements for future success. The statement(s) used to articulate the standards and competencies focus on critical aspects of student development that counseling professionals want to impact.

Counseling curriculum activities, organized in a developmentally appropriate scope and sequence, must be aligned with CBA standards and competency statements to ensure that students are provided with quality learning opportunities to achieve them.

These opportunities are delivered through the counseling curriculum—an integrated set of planned interventions with students that enables them to acquire knowledge, develop skills and embrace attitudes/behaviors that lead to success. Assessment processes and instruments to determine student progress toward stated results are defined for each curriculum activity. It is important to note that students also work toward many of the defined competencies outside of the planned counseling program. The counseling curriculum is viewed as the primary delivery system for standards-based activities because it is a defined set of core activities that is delivered to all students and is most capable of enabling uniform assessment of student progress toward the student standards.

STUDENT ASSESSMENT

Standards are end results to be achieved. Student standards articulate what knowledge, skills, attitudes and behaviors (aggregate of competency statements) students are expected to achieve by the time they graduate from high school. Standards and their related competency statements provide the criteria by which student proficiency and achievement can be determined.

Student assessments should be seen as part of the overall student evaluation process. According to the Joint Committee on Standards for Educational Evaluation (2003),

> Definition of Student Evaluation: The process of systematically collecting and interpreting information that can be used (1) to inform students and their parents/guardians about the progress they are making toward attaining the knowledge, skills, attitudes and behaviors to be learned or acquired; and, (2) to inform the various personnel who make educational decisions (instructional, diagnostic, placement, promotion, graduation) about students. (p. 232)

A CBA incorporates a K–12 construct-based assessment system that enables school counselors to design and implement their programs based on educational excellence, and enables them to monitor and guide student progress toward achieving the school counseling standards.

Proficiency is a function of measuring progress that places individuals on a spectrum of "no progress" to "achieving or exceeding the expected result." The term answers the question: To what extent is the competency or standard achieved? Rigorous and measurable student standards/competencies are critical to the school counseling profession. Without them, it is impossible to produce compelling evidence that demonstrates the positive impact of the school counseling program on student success.

STRATEGIC, ANNUAL AND PERSONAL PLANNING

Implementing a school counseling program requires well-developed plans. Four types of plans are used in a CBA. Strategic plans look three to five years into the future and establish the strategic direction of the school counseling program. These are best developed at the district level. Each school develops an annual school-specific plan for implementing the school counseling program during the current or upcoming year. Counselor-supervisor agreements focus on counselors and their supervisors/evaluators clearly defining results to be achieved by the end of the school year, developing action plans and ensuring measures that can accurately measure progress toward the stated goals. Finally, individual counselors are also encouraged to develop a plan for achieving results that outlines what they personally plan to do to deliver the CBA program during the school year.

PROGRAM IMPLEMENTATION AND EVALUATION

Data must be gathered about the impact of implementing a CBA. Formative assessments and summative evaluations monitor progress in implementing the program. Process, perception and results data are all used in the school counseling data management system.

DATA MANAGEMENT

If the standard specifies the end result students are expected to achieve, then a way is needed to assess their progress toward the result and a way to determine when the results have been successfully achieved. In other words, concrete evidence needs to be produced that demonstrates student progress toward and achievement of the expected result.

A student is not required to achieve school counseling student standards in order to be promoted from one grade/level to the next or for graduation from high school. The primary use of the student standards is to define what students are expected to achieve in terms of knowledge acquisition, skill development and attitudes/behaviors that lead to success. Data sheds light on students' needs and offers school counselors powerful opportunities to have meaningful interactions with their students by guiding their progress along the learning continuum.

A CBA is grounded in data-based decision making (DBDM) that uses data to establish student need, identify and deliver appropriate interventions, and evaluate the impact of implementing the interventions. Data are required to understand and effectively address students' learning needs and provide valuable information to help students improve their capacity to learn. Data are also used to provide vital information on the efficacy of the CBA school counseling program (Are the expected results for the program being achieved?).

HOW THE TERMS IN THE LANGUAGE SET RELATE

The key terms discussed above are all part of a process that enables school counselors to build a CBA program, implement it and evaluate its impact. Figure 2.1 shows how the chapters in the book address key aspects of a CBA.

The *CBA Toolkit* provides knowledge exercises, templates and presentations to guide you through this process and help you achieve your desired results.

STANDARDS AND COMPETENCIES ARE THE FOUNDATION OF THE CURRICULUM

Student results are defined as standards (end results) that students are expected to achieve by the time they graduate, and competencies (proficiency-building results) that define what students should be expected to know and demonstrate

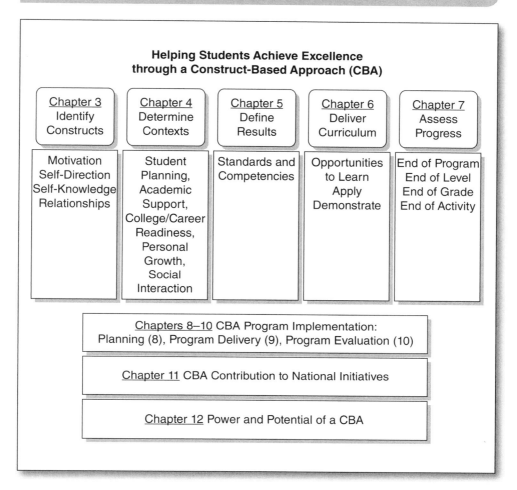

Figure 2.1 Helping Students Achieve Excellence

along the K–12 learning continuum. The standard and competency state-ments form the basis of a rigorous school counseling curriculum that pro-vides all students with quality opportunities to learn, apply what they are learning, and demonstrate what they know and can do as a result of their learning.

Assessments embedded in the curriculum and other assessments (e.g., end-of-level assessments) are used to determine students' progress toward and achievement of the competencies and standards. Data are gathered, ana-lyzed, and reported to students and their families. Data on the impact of implementing a construct-based program on student achievement are gener-ated and reported to those who need it to make informed decisions about the quality of the program and its delivery.

CONNECTING CHAPTER 2 TO TOOLKIT CONSTRUCTION SITE 1

The Toolkit is designed to help you first build a construct-based approach for your school counseling program and then to implement your CBA.

Chapters 2–5 in this book (*Achieving Excellence*) explore four critical areas needed to define student excellence: a) Chapter 2 proposes a simple language set to use when discussing a CBA, b) Chapter 3 provides research supporting the selection of four constructs as the basis of a CBA, c) Chapter 4 shows how the constructs are contextualized in terms of essential school counseling processes in which all students participate and d) Chapter 5 proposes CBA school counseling student standards and competencies that all students are expected to achieve.

Construction Site 1 combines the foci of these four areas to help you clearly define standards of student excellence in a CBA program (what students are expected to know and demonstrate as a result of the CBA).

As a result of completing Construction Site 1 tasks, you can expect to learn and do the following:

✓ Learn about the importance of a clearly defined language set in discussing student excellence.

✓ Learn key CBA concepts and vocabulary with concise definitions to aid in articulating and communicating a CBA.

Looking forward to working with you at Toolkit Construction Site 1!

3 Research-Based Constructs

Scenario 1

The counselors of Oak School District were upset to hear rumors that the School Board was considering reducing the school counseling ranks by one counselor in each of the middle and high schools and all of the elementary school counselors to help balance the budget in a tight fiscal year. The Director of Counseling met with them and urged them to demonstrate with data the impact they have on school initiatives, such as improving attendance and graduation rates. The counselors organized their efforts and utilized collective data to develop a PowerPoint presentation on the good work they were doing in their respective schools.

The night of the School Board meeting dedicated to discussing the elimination of school counseling positions, all of the counselors were present. The Director had signed up to be on the agenda to present the PowerPoint with representatives from the school counselors to assist him. The presentation demonstrated counselor interventions that supported an increase in attendance at each of the schools, as well as a decrease in out-of-school suspensions. The school counselors also offered data showing that some of their interventions helped reduce student retentions in middle school. The School Board expressed its admiration for the work of the school counselors and congratulated them on their good work. They then voted to reduce the school counseling positions as planned, citing the difficult fiscal situation.

Scenario 2

The counselors of Oak School District were upset to hear rumors that the School Board was considering reducing the school counseling ranks by one counselor in each of the middle and high schools and all of the elementary school counselors to help balance the budget in a tight fiscal year. They met with their Director of Counseling to strategize on their response to this threat. Having established a Construct-Based Approach (CBA) to developing their program district-wide, they felt strongly that they could convince the School Board of the value that their program added to the district's efforts to improve the education of every child. They put together folders for each member of the Board that included research on the constructs, the scope and sequence of their program at each level, and a copy of a PowerPoint presentation they planned to present at the next School Board meeting.

At the Board meeting, the Director and two school counselors presented the PowerPoint presentation and answered questions the Board members had on the research the counselors had provided. The school counselors were compelling as they made their case about how important the constructs are for every child and that nowhere else in the education program were they as focused and deliberately taught to every student. The School Board expressed their admiration for the work of the school counselors, and some members of the Board explained that they had no prior knowledge of the importance of the school counseling program. The Board discussed the value of the school counselors' program in helping the district meet its mission. They then voted to not reduce school counseling positions for the upcoming year. They did, however, invite the school counselors to give an update on their efforts at a Board meeting in six months.

Reflections

The value of research that shows evidence of making a difference in the education of children is very powerful. School counselors can use the research that backs the construct-based approach to school counseling as evidence that the curriculum we teach students contributes to their success in school and in life.

DEFINITION OF "RESEARCH-BASED"

In education today, it is very popular to claim that a professional practice is "research-based." Such claims are typically made without clearly defining what "research-based" means. When we say that the Construct-Based Approach (CBA) to school counseling is "research-based," we mean that the standards were written to reflect student abilities, competencies, capabilities and skills that 1) have been established by research in educational and developmental psychology to be strongly related to students' academic achievement and later success in life, and 2) are acquired or perfected through experience and learning. We chose lines of research connected to student competencies that were primarily within the domain of the work of counselors—that fell within the academic, personal/social and career development domains of school counseling practice.

Unique Role of School Counselors

It is important to note that different types of educators make different types of contributions to students' abilities to achieve and succeed. While all good educators are invested in the holistic development of students, each attends to different facets of the educational experience which, when coordinated well, catalyze maximal learning and development. Classroom teachers, for example, attend more to the obvious, observable and measureable aspects of achievement. They focus on the facts, concepts and processes that reflect mastery of a particular area of knowledge and enact effective instructional techniques that maximize students' opportunities to acquire knowledge and expertise. In contrast, counselors help students develop the knowledge, skills, attitudes, beliefs and habits of mind that enable them to profit maximally from their instructional opportunities and experiences.

NEW FOCUS ON PERSONAL, SOCIAL AND LIFE SKILLS

Over the past 25 years, the importance of these types of abilities and skills has been repeatedly noted. For example, in 1990, the U.S. Secretary of Labor initiated a commission to identify the skills that people need in the world of work. In addition to the basic skills in reading, writing and mathematics, the Commission identified a number of critically important skills that are clearly within the traditional foci of school counselors. Such skills include listening to others, participating effectively in groups, understanding other's emotions, dealing with cultural diversity, managing oneself, assuming responsibility, managing one's own self-esteem, decision making and problem solving (Secretary's Commission on Achieving Necessary Skills, 1991).

More recently the Partnership for 21st Century Skills (P21) has identified a set of skills that they see as necessary for success in the complex, changing, globally interconnected context that shapes modern life (Trilling & Fadel, 2009). These skills are being used in many states to focus and direct educational reform initiatives. The P21 skill framework includes a strong focus on life and career skills that include multiple abilities (e.g., maintaining flexibility and adaptability, taking initiative and being self-directed, managing differences and working collaboratively with others, accepting responsibility and being accountable, leading others, acting responsibly in the interests of the larger community).

Similarly, from the education policy perspective, noted economist and Nobel laureate James Heckman (Heckman & Krueger, 2003) has studied the factors affecting the achievement gap in the United States and concluded that both "cognitive" (academic skills) and "non-cognitive skills" (e.g., self-direction skills, social engagement skills, self-regulation skills, openness, conscientious-ness, pro-social orientation, social skills) are responsible for the gap and that programs that focus on helping students develop their non-cognitive skills are an essential component of effective gap reduction approaches.

Relatedly, Levin (2012) summarized research on the relationships between the development of intrapersonal and interpersonal skills (labeled "non-cognitive skills") and the quality and productivity of the labor force. He noted that there is a stronger relationship between students' non-cognitive skills and their earning level as an adult than there is between students' achievement test scores and their later earnings levels.

Furthermore he found that elementary, middle and high schools can also significantly improve non-cognitive factors if there is a focus on implementing "purposeful interventions" targeted in these areas. Based on the research evidence, Levin suggested that: 1) schools should be commit-ted to purposeful interventions that promote students' development of "motivation, self-discipline, persistence, cooperation, self-presentation, tolerance, respect, and other non-cognitive dimensions"; 2) this focus on non-cognitive factors should be evident in early childhood programs, ele-mentary schools, middle schools and high schools; and 3) governments should invest in the development of measurement of non-cognitive success factors to monitor the performance of schools.

Recently, ACT (2011) published a summary of important academic behaviors for success in school, and for college and career readiness and success. The ACT review indicated that, consistent with Robbins et al. (2004), the academic behaviors that are important for student success can be grouped into three broad areas:

- "Motivation includes personal characteristics that help students succeed academically by focusing and maintaining energies on goal-directed activities."

- "Social Engagement includes interpersonal factors that influence stu-dents' successful integration into their environment."

- "Self-Regulation includes the thinking processes and emotional responses of students that govern how well they monitor, regulate, and control their behavior related to school and learning."

We have used the ACT schema to help organize the CBA. The factors included in the ACT review are strongly related to achievement, malleable, and within the scope and function of school counselors to address.

School counselors provide a necessary complement to the work of teach-ers because students need to learn to develop their non-cognitive skills in order to profit maximally from a rigorous curriculum and effective instruction. The construct-based school counseling student standards are focused on these non-cognitive skills that actually might better be thought of as self-direction or self-determination skills. The research literatures in educational and developmental psychology contain several lines of research that relate directly to the question of exactly which skill and competencies students should develop in this interaction with the school counseling program in order to achieve academically and be successful. Some of the major lines of research are briefly summarized below.

MOTIVATION

The study of motivation is the study of the forces that compel action and direct the behavior of individuals. It is one of the most researched topics in psychology. We know that students differ in what they find motivating (e.g., sports vs. academics) and in the apparent intensity of their motivated behavior. School counselors can help students develop the knowledge, skills and work habits that all students need to be successful. Some students, however, do not connect with school on a motivational level and therefore fail to thrive in the public school environment. These students do not find school intrinsically interesting and do not seem to make the connection between academic achievement and future success. They are frequently described by educators as "unmotivated." If public schools are to be successful in helping all students achieve, educators need to develop approaches that will help all students develop the motivation to expend sustained and persistent effort on learning tasks that appear far removed from their ultimate rewards and benefits. Helping students develop ways to understand their personal motivational structures and to motivate their own behavior is critically important in helping them achieve in school and succeed in life.

Achievement Motivation is an area of psychological theory and research that focuses on understanding human motivations to succeed (Atkinson & Feather, 1966; McClelland, 1965) and reflects an important pillar for the CBA. Research in achievement motivation has validated the importance of distinguishing between intrinsic motivation and extrinsic motivation (Pintrich & Schunk, 2002).

Intrinsic motivation refers to the things that an individual finds to be motivating by their very nature. *Extrinsic motivation* refers to the things that are done to achieve an arbitrary reward. For example, students may enjoy writing stories so much so that they write stories in their spare time at home (intrinsic motivation) and at the same time they will practice solving math problems only because they want to get a good grade on the tests (extrinsic motivation).

It is important that all students understand what things they find to be intrinsically interesting and cultivate and develop their intrinsic interests. Areas of intrinsic interest reflect appropriate career directions and academic specializations. It is likewise important that all students identify the tasks that they must master that are not intrinsically interesting. In these areas they will need to learn to apply self-motivational strategies to direct and sustain their learning behavior.

Self-Determination Theory and research provides an important perspective on how to help students develop the motivation to engage in learning-related tasks that are not intrinsically interesting to them. Self-Determination Theory (Ryan & Deci, 2000) suggests that there are actually several different types of situations in which extrinsic motivation operates. In *externally regulated* situations, students are motivated exclusively by the rewards and punishments that occur as a consequence of their actions.

Students develop little personal investment in these actions and will not perform them unless rewards or punishments are likely to result. In *introjected regulation* situations, students are motivated by a desire for the approval of others. They will engage in learning if they perceive that it will result in enhanced regard for them from important others. In *regulation through identification* situations, students engage in activities that they have consciously examined and have identified as having value for them. Finally, in *integrated regulation* situations, students engage in activities because the activities have been integrated into their self-concept and life goals.

As an example, students may study math because their parents will give them $10 if they do well on the test (external), because they want the teacher to think well of them (introjection), because they are certain that they will need to know math in order to get a good job (identification) or because they see themselves as a young engineer who needs to understand math (integration).

Self-Determination Theory and research suggest regulation through identification and through integration reflect higher levels of internalization by the student, which is manifested in a greater sense of autonomy, greater effort, greater persistence and higher performance (especially on difficult and/or complex tasks). Internalization is promoted by learning environments that tap into students' basic needs to feel competent, autonomous and related to others (Deci, Eghrari, Patrick, & Leone, 1994).

If counselors are able to promote students' internalization of motivation by helping them recognize the value of their school learning and by helping them develop a positive future identity into which the academic learning is integrated, higher levels of self-motivated work to master the academic material and consequently higher levels of academic achievement will result.

Possible Selves Theory and research reflect another important motivational underpinning of the CBA. Possible Selves Theory and its related research base (Markus & Nurius, 1986) provide a potentially powerful framework for this technology. Possible Selves Theory is an extension of Self-Concept Theory. Similar to other approaches in this tradition, Possible Selves Theory emphasizes the impact that a student's self-definition has on school behavior. The special contribution of Possible Selves Theory is its focus on the motivational power of students' views of themselves in the future. Students' views of the selves that they would hope to become, fear they will become and expect to become can be powerful motivators for present school behavior.

> Possible selves are the ideal selves that we would very much like to become. They are also the selves that we could become and are afraid of becoming. The possible selves that are hoped for might include the successful self, the creative self, the rich self, the thin self, or the loved and admired self, whereas, the dreaded possible selves could be the alone self, the depressed self, the incompetent self, the alcoholic self, the unemployed self, or the bag lady self. (Markus & Nurius, 1986, p. 954)

Students' motivation to engage in effortful learning in school is related to how vividly they can picture different possible selves, the nature of their possible selves, and the connections students perceive between school behavior and either achieving a positive self or avoiding a negative self. Possible selves are projections about the future that are rooted in students' present and past experiences. Both positive and negative possible selves reflect what students have come to believe are actually possible for them. The nature of students' possible selves is strongly influenced by their culture, class, socioeconomic circumstances, family environment, and personal experiences of success or failure in school. Students' possible selves are also shaped by role models and exposure to media.

Several studies document the relationships between students' possible selves and their achievement and school-related behavior (Anderman, Anderman, & Griesinger, 1999; Leondari, Syngollitou, & Kiosseoglou, 1998; Oyserman, Gant, & Anger, 1995; Oyserman & Markus, 1990). In addition, several studies have found that possible-selves-based interventions have positive effects on student achievement (Day, Borkowski, Ponzo, & Howsepian, 1994; Oyserman, Bybee, & Terry, 2006). Students will be more motivated if they have a clear and vivid picture image of their future and see the relationships between their immediate day-to-day choices and behavior and their long-term vision.

Helping students understand their motivation and patterns, cultivate their intrinsic interests, create a vivid vision of their possible futures, and see how their immediate choices and behavior relate to their long-term vision is clearly an important part of the work of school counselors. Students who are able to do these things are much more likely to achieve and succeed than those students who cannot.

Goal setting reflects the specific skills associated with directing and maintaining effort toward the achievement of goals. Goal setting is a particularly effective method for helping students develop and maintain motivation in school. Self-directed learners need to develop specific skills in self-regulating their learning behavior toward their self-chosen goals (Zimmerman, 1990). Goal setting is a powerful tool to help students self-regulate their learning.

Research has consistently demonstrated that effective goal setting results in enhanced motivation and performance (Locke, 1996, 2001; Morisano, Hirsh, Peterson, Pihl, & Shore, 2010). Learning how to set goals that are ambitious, challenging, personally meaningful and attainable is an important prerequisite for academic achievement and lifelong success. The CBA indicates that all students learn effective goal setting as part of their portfolio of strategies to promote learning through the self-regulation of motivation.

SELF-KNOWLEDGE AND SELF-DIRECTION

Self-knowledge refers to the understanding people have about their own abilities, values, preferences and skills that is a necessary precondition for effective self-regulation. Self-direction refers to the capabilities of people to direct their own lives based on their understandings of themselves, others, and the world and their skill in managing their own learning, motivation and behavior.

Self-directed individuals actively manage their own lives rather than passively following the path of least resistance. Self-directed individuals have been described as having an internal "locus of control" (Rotter, 1990) and as having a strong sense of "self-efficacy" (Bandura, 1997). This means that such individuals are more likely to believe that they can alter the world by their actions and are capable of acting effectively on the world. Consequently, they are more likely to initiate action proactively, persist during adversity and show resilience in the face of failure. Acquiring essential self-knowledge and learning to be self-directed are important and desirable goals for all students and should be a focus for the work of all school counselors.

Metacognitive awareness is the introspective ability to observe one's own mental functions, thoughts, and behavior and draw useful inferences (e.g., about strengths, weaknesses, interests, motivational patterns) to guide learning and decision making (Flavell, 1987). Research indicates that students can develop their metacognitive awareness through school-based interventions (Schraw, 1998).

Much of the work of school counselors involves helping students acquire metacognitive awareness to guide their own learning, career development and social relationships. Traditionally, counselors have helped students develop metacognitive awareness of their interests, values, abilities, learning styles, temperament and personality—all of which promote effective learning, self-direction and decision making.

Attributional style is one additional important area of metacognitive awareness. When individuals experience a success or a failure they immediately (and sometimes automatically) attribute the outcome to a cause. The cause that is selected can have a profound effect on future behavior. Attributions of causation affect motivation and influence whether or not individuals try something and whether or not they will persist if they initially experience hardship or failure (Wiener, 1974).

For example, if students believe that their grade on a test is determined by a "powerful other" (e.g., "I'll get a good grade if the teacher likes me"), by luck (e.g., "I'll get a good grade if it's my lucky day") or by unchangeable aspects of themselves (e.g., "I'll get a good grade if I'm intelligent enough"), they are unlikely to be motivated to study for the test. If, on the other hand, they believe that the outcome of the test is largely determined by things they can actually do to make a difference (e.g., "I'll get a good grade on the test if I study hard enough") they will be motivated to act.

Similarly, students who have explanatory styles that attribute success and failure to uncontrollable causes are less likely to be optimistic and more likely to be depressed. In addition to being related to learning, attribution style is related to optimism (Seligman, 2006), as well as to psychological resilience and depression (Seligman & Nolen-Hoeksema, 1987). A negative attribution style also predisposes students to self-handicapping behavior—the substitution of maladaptive behavior for achievement-oriented behavior in order to prevent self-esteem loss associated with anticipated "unavoidable" failures (Jones & Berglas, 1978). Clearly, learning to make accurate causal attributions and recognize and compensate for biases introduced by one's own explanatory style is an important aspect of metacognitive skills. They should be a focus of school counseling programs, given the strong relationship between explanatory style, achievement, resilience and mental health.

Self-directed learning refers to a family of related approaches to education that recognize that learners need to be taught how to develop skills in the effective use of learning strategies while they are learning academic concepts and content (Ambrose, Bridges, DiPietro, Lovett & Norman, 2010). All students need to learn and to learn how to learn.

Students are more likely to take initiative and responsibility for directing their own learning if they are active self-directed learners. The development of self-directed learning is enhanced when students exercise choice in what they learn and when classroom learning is connected to students' personal interests (Corno, 1992). Self-directed learners show an awareness of their responsibility in choosing what they learn, are curious and open to try new things, view problems as challenges, desire change, enjoy learning, are more persistent, are self-confident and are goal-oriented (Mardziah, 2001). They are more effective learners with a stronger commitment to lifelong learning. Through interactions with the counseling programs, all students are encouraged to identify their own life directions, make academic choices consistent with these directions and connect their classroom learning to their life goals.

Self-regulation refers to an individual's ability to alter his own internal states in order to facilitate effective functioning. The ability to regulate both one's attention and emotion is an important factor in both achievement in school, in well-being and in later success (ACT, 2011; DuPaul & Stoner, 2003; Graziano, Reavis, Keane, & Calkins, 2007; Gumora & Arsenio, 2002).

Children need to learn how to direct their own attention and modulate emotional states related to fear, anxiety, anger and depression. Children who have self-regulation difficulties often show interpersonal problems in addition to academic difficulties and without intervention are on the track toward chronic underachievement, stunted social interest and dissatisfaction. Effective interventions have been developed to teach self-regulation in a wide range of domains including, for example: attention (Reid, Trout, & Schartz, 2005; Semple, Lee, Rosa, & Miller, 2010), anger management (Fraser et al., 2005), stress management (McCraty, Atkinson, Tomasino, Goelitz, & Mayrovitz, 1999) and anxiety (Rapee, Schniering & Hudson, 2009).

The majority of these effective approaches use some form of cognitive-behavioral skills training to teach students how to control their own internal processes and to modulate their own internal emotional states. By enabling all students to regulate their own attention and emotional states, school counselors promote the development of essential skills necessary for learning, persistence, resilience, and effective and satisfying social interactions.

Executive Functions Theory and research have, in recent years, extended our understanding of the neuropsychological underpinnings of complex cognitive processes related to self-regulation and have led to clear definitions of these processes. Cognitive processes that act to control and regulate other cognitive processes can be said to serve an executive function (Elliot, 2003). Brown (2006) has developed a theoretical model of executive functions that suggests there are six discriminable categories of processes: 1) activation-related processes (related to the organization, prioritization and initiation of activities), 2) focusing-related processes (related to sustaining and shifting attention to tasks), 3) effort-related processes (related to regulation alertness and sustaining effort on activities), 4) emotion-related processes (related to managing frustration and promoting positive emptions that affect task completion), 5) memory-related processes (related to recalling information and using working memory) and 6) action-related processes (related to monitoring and regulation of one's own actions).

Research evidence indicates that relatively late-developing brain structures (especially the prefrontal areas of the frontal cortex) are necessary for the proper expression of executive functions (Alvarez & Emory, 2006). The discovery that the maturation of these brain structures occur late in humans and is extended well into adolescence (Casey, Jones, & Hare, 2008) has led to the suggestion that the maturation of these structures permits the progressive development of self-regulation observed through childhood and adolescence and explains why many adolescents shown "deficits" in executive function-related capabilities and behavior.

The U.S. Department of Health and Human Services Office of Population Affairs (2013) indicates, for example, that incomplete maturation of prefrontal cortex–related executive functions explains why many adolescents have difficulty with

- focusing attention,

- organizing thoughts and problem solving,

- foreseeing and weighing possible consequences of behavior,

- considering the future and making predictions,

- forming strategies and planning,

- balancing short-term rewards with long-term goals,

- shifting/adjusting behavior when situations change,

- controlling impulse and delaying gratification,

- modulating intense emotions,

- inhibiting inappropriate behavior and initiating appropriate behavior, and

- considering multiple streams of information simultaneously when faced with complex and challenging information.

Similarly, executive function deficits (and associated problems with brain development) have been implicated as important causal factors in several developmental disabilities including attention deficit disorder (Willcutt, Doyle, Nigg, Faraone, & Pennington, 2005). In addition, the development of executive functions in young children has been demonstrated to be related to both school readiness and early academic achievement (Blair, 2002; Blair & Diamond, 2008; Blair & Razza, 2007; Clark, Pritchard, & Woodward, 2010; Willoughby, Wirth, Blair, Greenberg, & The Family Life Project Investigators, 2012).

Research on effective interventions to improve children's executive functions is still in its infancy. A wide range of specific interventions has been identified that includes specially designed computer training, exercise, mindfulness training and school-based curricula. However, it is likely that these specific interventions are more effective when embedded in a broader educational emphasis on the development of students' social and emotional learning (Diamond & Lee, 2011). In the next few years, research on how to promote the development of executive functions and remediate deficits in executive functions is likely to make important contributions to effective practice in school counseling.

RELATIONSHIPS

To learn and to live effectively require good social skills. To learn effectively, students need to establish and maintain productive, collaborative, social relationships with teachers and with peers. Students need to learn how to work in classrooms, work groups and teams to achieve common objectives. Research indicates that there is a strong link between social competence and academic achievement (Payton et al., 2008). Social skills have also repeatedly been identified as an essential ability for work and career success (Secretary's Commission on Achieving Necessary Skills, 1991; Trilling & Fadel, 2009).

Individual achievement needs to be grounded in social interest and a commitment to working to improve one's local, national and global communities. Otherwise, the pursuit of individual achievement can lead to self-absorption and the unbridled pursuit of self-interest at the expense of others. Consequently, the CBA suggests that all students need to develop the broader social understanding that allows them to recognize current inequities in society and the commitment to work for a more equitable and just society.

Social skills have been defined by Walker (1983) as "a set of competencies that a) allow an individual to initiate and maintain positive social relationships, b) contribute to peer acceptance and to a satisfactory school adjustment, and c) allow an individual to cope effectively with the larger social environment" (p. 27). Social skills are built on a foundation of social and emotional learning.

In order to demonstrate good social skills, students need to recognize their emotions, recognize the emotion of others, manage their emotions, develop empathy and perspective-taking abilities, establish positive relationships, make good decisions in social contexts, and manage challenging social situations constructively and ethically (Zins, Weissbert, Wang, & Walberg, 2004).

Research also indicates that social skills can be taught effectively in school context (Beelmann, Pfingsten, & Losel, 1994; Honig & Wittmer, 1996) and that a number of effective social skills programs exist (see Gibbs, Potter, & Goldstein, 1995; McGinnis & Goldstein, 1997; Walker, 1983). The CBA suggests that all students should develop good social skills through their interactions with the school counseling program.

Help seeking is a critically important social skill that is strongly related to success in school and in life (Nelson-Le Gall, 1981). When students encounter inevitable problems associated with mastering school material, engaging in self-initiated help-seeking will help them learn and achieve. In order to seek help effectively, students need to be able to recognize that they need help, decide what type of help they need, decide who can provide that help and effectively approach that individual (or individuals) to elicit their help (Nelson Le-Gall, 1985; Newman, 1994).

Help-seeking is an important component of self-regulated learning that is enacted in the social context of schools (Newman, 1994; Zimmerman & Martinez-Pons, 1988). If students learn effective help-seeking skills they will be prepared not only to address their immediate problems in school but also to become better able to solve problems throughout their lives by seeking needed assistance. The CBA suggests that all students should develop good help-seeking skills through their interactions with the school counseling program.

Critical consciousness (Kincheloe & Steinberg, 1993) is a form of critical thinking that allows individuals to recognize and understand the relationships between power, intergroup oppression and social justice at the community, societal and international levels. When individuals exercise critical consciousness they explore questions related to human dignity, freedom, authority, social responsibility and personal purpose.

Educating for Social Justice is a movement within the field of education that focuses on the development, implementation and evaluation of procedures, approaches and techniques associated with teaching critical consciousness and pro-social action. In the past, most of the research in this area has been focused on the development of critical consciousness in teachers and other public school personnel (see Bell, 1997; Darling-Hammond, French, & Garcia-Lopez, 2002). Recent research has begun to focus on effective techniques for social justice education for public school students (Brooks & Thompson, 2005; Lalas, 2007). A number of interesting and potentially powerful approaches have been developed (see Beale, 2004; Lalas, 2007; Lucas, 2005; McLaughlin & DeVoogd, 2004).

The CBA indicates that all students should develop the ability to understand diversity, recognize inequity and act in ways to promote a more just society. Given the current state of the art, this will require practicing counselors to use the existing research base to develop the effective social justice education interventions. Relatedly, school counseling researchers ought to be involved in researching the effectiveness of these interventions and assessing the value of and benefits associated with students' participation in social justice education in schools.

CONCLUSIONS

The CBA is aligned with important areas of research within educational and developmental psychology, which identify specific abilities, skills and attitudes that are known through research to be strongly linked to achievement in school and to success in life after school. School counselors can use the CBA to focus their work on the improvement of students' motivation, self-knowledge, self-direction and social skills in the context of enhanced social responsibility.

Through their interactions with the school counseling program, all students will learn to direct their own lives, contribute to the good of society, and benefit maximally from their classroom instruction and educational opportunities. An additional benefit of aligning the CBA with the established research literature is that many of the measures developed in these literatures can be used to evaluate specific school counseling interventions and develop more general measures of standards attainment and program effectiveness. While there is still work to do in this area, establishing a CBA that explicitly links to major lines of research on student success is a major step forward in establishing measureable outcomes for the school counseling profession.

Chapter 3

CONSTRUCTION ZONE

Thinking Hard Hats Required

CONNECTING CHAPTER 3 TO TOOLKIT CONSTRUCTION SITE 1

Two phrases that are central to any discussion about quality school counseling programs and how to improve them are "research-based" and "evidence-based." These phrases signal the importance of basing our program design, delivery and evaluation on proven approaches, strategies and methodologies. That which research suggests school counselors can and should be doing ought to be a powerful influence in shaping the school counseling profession.

Achieving Excellence is an effort to understand what research from educational and developmental psychology and school counseling suggest are those areas of student learning and development in which school counselors can have the greatest potential for impact on student development, achievement and future success. Our review of the research yielded the four constructs of motivation, self-direction, self-knowledge and motivation, which form the basis of the CBA. It is important for school counselors to be aware of the research on which their programs are based.

Chapter 3 also uses Toolkit Construction Site 1 ("Defining Student Excellence") as the four research-based constructs become one of the five building blocks for developing a CBA that can be integrated into your own school counseling program.

As a result of completing Construction Site 1 tasks, you can expect to learn and do the following:

✓ Learn about the research that yielded the constructs of motivation, self-direction, self-knowledge and relationships as a major building block for a CBA.

✓ Learn how to make the most out of research.

✓ Identify and explore the constructs on which to build your CBA.

✓ Practice viewing student needs, learning and development through the filters of the four constructs.

Looking forward to working with you at Toolkit Construction Site 1!

4 Relevant Contexts for K–12 School Counseling Programs

Scenario 1

The superintendent, in a directive to principals, recommended that to improve student test scores and meet state and federal requirements, schools improve their focus on student academic support, college and career readiness, and student plans for the post-secondary world. The principals turned the directive over to the school counselors and told them to deal with these areas in their school counseling program. The counselors, who were feeling stretched to the limit with all of their current responsibilities, felt completely overwhelmed and wondered how they could take on these additional initiatives. They didn't know how to get started.

Scenario 2

The superintendent, in a directive to principals, recommended that to improve student test scores and meet state and federal requirements, schools improve their focus on student academic support, college and career readiness, and student plans for the post-secondary world. The principal of the high school met with his school counselors to discuss this. The counselors explained how their program was based on research-backed educational constructs that would help students develop the knowledge and skills to scaffold their learning. They believed that each of these initiatives could be considered a filter through which to view their program. The curriculum, based on these constructs, supported all of the initiatives. They assured the principal that they would use data-based decisions to maximize the impact on students. One problem the school counselors had faced was having continual access to students to deliver curriculum. The principal worked out a plan with the counselors so that every student in each grade would benefit from the school counseling program and explained the effort to all faculty at the next faculty meeting. The school counselors implemented their program as planned and at the end of the school year demonstrated with data the actual results they attained for students.

Reflections

When school counselors can articulate the research that backs the constructs on which their program was developed, they are more convincing that implementation to every student will have a positive impact on achievement. When new policies or initiatives are introduced to the district, they often fit into a construct-based program with a simple shift in focus.

FROM CONSTRUCTS TO CONTEXTS

The research-based constructs identified in Chapter 3 (motivation, self-direction, self-knowledge, relationships) point to four areas of student learning and development in which school counselors can have a significant impact. It is possible to develop a Construct-Based Approach (CBA) to school counseling wherein these four areas become a primary focus of the school counseling program.

The constructs are a primary filter when thinking about school counselors interacting with students. A CBA focuses on helping students achieve excellence by setting rigorous standards and competencies, having high expectations for every student, delivering a standards-based school counseling curriculum and assessing student progress toward school counseling student standards and competencies.

These constructs are the primary filters used to articulate student standards (the end-of-program results students are expected to achieve by the time they graduate from high school). For example, as a result of participating in the school counseling program, students are expected to be highly motivated, self-directed learners who are knowledgeable about themselves, engaged in meaningful relationships and developing as contributing members of society.

How do we get from four research-based constructs to the everyday delivery of a school counseling program? The constructs are a significant filter, but in and of themselves they lack immediacy, relevance and meaningfulness in the counselor's life. In short, the constructs lack "contexts" in which the four constructs become important in terms of identifying student needs and taking appropriate action in a timely fashion. Relevant contexts are the real-life processes students need to successfully navigate the school counseling program and graduate having demonstrated that they are highly motivated and self-directed, knowing who they are and how to relate to others in meaningful ways.

COMPETENCY STATEMENTS EMERGE FROM CONTEXTS

Learning occurs in contexts, not in a vacuum. It is therefore important to understand those contexts in which school counselors and students interact that are critical to student development and achievement. Five "relevant contexts" are addressed in this book: a) student planning, b) academic support, c) college and career readiness, d) personal growth and e) social interaction. This is not intended to be an exhaustive list, but it does serve to focus attention on areas critical to all students.

Standard statements articulate the end results that students are expected to achieve by the time they graduate from high school. Like constructs, standard statements are very general and do not specify any details about knowledge and skill performance requirements. Competency statements are needed to add specificity (concrete examples) regarding what students should know and demonstrate.

Competency statements identify what students are expected to know and do along the K–12 learning continuum. They focus on the specific knowledge, skills and behaviors/attitudes that enable student growth and support student achievement. Whereas standards are general statements that articulate what students are expected to achieve as a result of the entire school counseling program, competencies are statements that are directly tied to essential contexts in which students are engaged while participating in the school counseling program. Competency statements only become relevant and meaningful in terms of context. Without context, there is no way of relating what is being taught to what is emerging in the biographies of the students and the adults who are guiding them.

CONTEXTS CONSIST OF ESSENTIAL PROCESSES

Each context can be understood in terms of the essential processes in which students are expected to become proficient. Helping students acquire knowledge about the processes, and develop skills for applying the knowledge in specific contexts, is the primary purpose of a competency statement. A list of essential processes is provided for each of the five contexts addressed in this chapter. The lists are not intended to be exhaustive but to serve as a beginning point for learning how to personally develop meaningful competency statements.

ACADEMIC SUPPORT

Academic support can take many forms, but all of them share a common result they would like to achieve: every student graduating from high school is prepared to enter the post-secondary world and be successful. Two types of academic support are noted here: a) direct student contact and b) collaborating with teachers.

A CBA focuses on the whole child. Every child has learning processes and learning needs based on how well they have mastered the processes. Professional school counselors identify learning needs and work collaboratively with teachers to address them. Through a sharing of knowledge and expertise, school counselors contribute much to support student achievement, particularly in the areas of helping students learn how to learn, plan for their futures and cope with their social and emotional development.

Academic support can come in the form of counselor-led interventions wherein school counselors interact directly with students. L. D. Webb, Brigman and Campbell (2005) reviewed studies examining the impact of counselor-led interventions on student achievement and behavior. They concluded that when school counselors use research-based interventions to develop critical skills associated with school success, the academic achievement and social competence of students is enhanced.

The authors also noted how essential it is for "counselors to use evidence-based practices that show results in academic achievement and social performance, areas that make a difference to decision makers" (L. D. Webb et al., 2005, p. 413).

Academic support of students can be enhanced through collaboration between counselors and teachers. Ian Brodie, a middle school counselor, posted "The Top 10 Ways School Counselors Can Support Teachers" (2012).

The 10 ways are a call to collaboration. Brodie recommends that teachers call on counselors to help them understand the whole student, give advice on effective strategies for working with students, address problems early, help integrate counseling into class lessons, provide appropriate professional development, provide an assessment of the severity of a problem and be a resource to handle difficult student problems. The 10 ways, like the CBA, encourages counselors and teachers to collaborate on lessons that help students meet competencies in both the content area and the CBA.

Other academic support activities can include inventories (e.g., learning styles, career interest, personality), study skills, executive function development, academic audits, career exploration, assistance in planning and referrals to other personnel/resources. In particular, school counselors have a special role in helping to address the metacognitive aspects of students' learning, and helping students learn about their own thinking and behavior patterns.

Just as the constructs are significant filters to use when implementing a CBA, the contexts are also filters that tie the constructs to real-life processes in which students are engaged through participation in the school counseling program. The academic support context allows school counselors to identify and deliver construct-based solutions to students' learning needs.

When the constructs and contexts are viewed together, they help in the design of authentic learning opportunities that will allow students to construct meaning for the learning experience and use it to progress into the future. For example, when looking at what school counselors do to support students' academic achievement, it is appropriate to ask how motivation relates to each of the processes identified above. What does motivation have to do with career interest inventories or career exploration? How does motivation influence student planning? By combining the construct and context filters, it is possible to look at the impact of the constructs in specific activities that must be successfully completed for students to graduate prepared for entry into the post-secondary world.

Student Planning (Individual Learning Plans)

Planning for one's future success is one of the most important life skills a CBA can offer students. Essential processes in the student planning context provide students with the learning targets and tools they will need to become proficient planners. For example, learning targets for planning can include a) learning a complete planning process, b) defining measureable results, c) developing, documenting and implementing action plans, d) coping with and overcoming barriers to learning, e) monitoring student progress and making adjustments, as needed, f) reflecting on one's experience and g) using the results to adjust learning plans.

Student planning is a central focus of a CBA program as the ability to plan is a key factor in getting a job and advancing up the career ladder. Planning proficiency is highly valued in the post-secondary world. School counselors are in a unique position to guide students through an individual planning process because of their training in the academic, career, personal and social developmental domains. From goal setting to self-reflection, school counselors have a high impact on student planning.

College and Career Readiness

Preparation for college and preparation for a career are increasingly viewed collectively. Academic and career have often been treated as separate entities that can be discussed apart from each other. Now the focus is on viewing them together, recognizing that one cannot be addressed without reference to the other. The following are considered to be among the essential processes that comprise college and career readiness.

A CBA expects students to be able to describe the relationship of school, work and future success, and be able to recognize and exhibit attitudes and behaviors that lead to success. An important aspect of this, as discussed in Chapter 3, involves students focusing on their possible future selves. A CBA promotes the development of a clear sense of what selves are possible for individual students, what is required to be successful and how the counselor can help facilitate each student's journey into the future. By focusing on learning about one's intrinsic and extrinsic motivations, understanding one's thinking and behavior patterns, becoming proficient planners and finding that right set of relationships that inspire creativity and life, students will enter the post-secondary world prepared for success.

Goal setting, action plan development, plan implementation, monitoring of progress and assessment of results are all addressed in a CBA. Individual Learning Plans (ILP) provide a context in which planning for one's future becomes an organizing principle for one's life. Exploration is another key theme in a CBA. The exploration is both internal (learning about one's self and how to self-regulate one's existence) and external (exploration of post-secondary opportunities).

Higher-order thinking, decision making and problem solving are meta-cognitive learning skills addressed by a CBA. School counselors help students to reason more effectively, make good decisions, systematically solve problems, and be able to look at situations and the world critically. These are essential skills because the decisions made will have a major impact on a student's future. Counselors help students make informed decisions regarding post-secondary opportunities and selection of educational and career pathways to pursue. Both academic and employability skills are addressed.

A useful filter for understanding the context of college and career readiness is the "Eight Components of College and Career Readiness Counseling," published by the College Board's National Office for School Counselor Advocacy (NOSCA, 2010).

The components are a systematic approach to helping school counselors prepare students to make informed decisions regarding life after high school. Students and families are encouraged to do early college planning. It is expected that students from underrepresented populations will especially benefit from focusing on these components.

The first component focuses on college aspirations and establishing a school culture that encourages and supports students being prepared for education and training in the post-secondary world. School counselors are instrumental in creating such a culture because of their pivotal role in preparing students for the college application process. The second component concerns a rigorous academic planning process to help students set goals related to further education and career choices.

The third component focuses on enrichment activities and getting students involved in extracurricular activities. Equal access to these opportunities must be made available to all students. Component four focuses on exploring college and career opportunities and making informed choices. The fifth components addresses college and career assessments of all students in terms of their preparation and performance in pursuit of post-secondary opportunities they wish to pursue.

The cost of higher education highly constrains many families who do not have funds available to pay for an education. Component six emphasizes the need to get as much information as possible to families so they understand how to make college affordable. The seventh component provides families with an understanding of the college and career admissions process and how to successfully navigate it. The eighth and final component focuses on the transition from high school through enrollment in college. The purpose is to connect students with resources to help support and facilitate the transition.

Personal Growth

School counselors are recognized as key agents of personalization in schools. They are seen as responsible adults who know their students well and whom students trust to help them with issues they face growing up. Much of the work school counselors do in this context involves students' self-image, barriers to their learning and behavioral issues that require guidance from a responsible adult. The following are considered to be among the essential processes in the personal growth context.

The CBA curriculum provides learning style and personality inventories to help students understand how they learn and how they can improve their learning processes. Curriculum activities focus on instilling positive learning habits in students while nurturing students' personal development. Activities designed to prevent future problems (e.g., bullying program, conflict resolution) are also incorporated into the curriculum, which is offered primarily through whole class and small group activities.

Those students who require one-on-one interventions are generally addressed through responsive (on demand) services in which student needs are addressed by the counselor or the student is referred to other resources. In a CBA, individual student needs, in part, are defined in terms of motivation, self-direction, self-knowledge and relationships. A CBA encourages the development of a strong self-concept and a clear sense of one's possible selves. A strong self-concept and respect for one's self can enhance students' respect for each other.

Social Interaction

Just as students are maturing as individuals, they are also growing up in relation to others. Being a guide to students as their individual biographies emerge in social interaction is another critical area in which school counselors can make a significant impact on students' well-being. The following are considered to be essential processes in the social interaction context.

The discussion on the Partnership for 21st Century Skills reveals a large number of social skills that are required for success in the post-secondary world. Students' ability to collaborate and work as a team member are in high demand by employers, as are the abilities to effectively communicate, make decisions and solve problems.

This "social interaction" context is addressed in large part by the "relationships" construct. Social interaction is required for success in the workplace as well as getting along with others and finding innovative ways to collaborate to achieve common goals. Social interaction skills can also be used to promote equity and social justice through implementing a CBA.

CONNECTING CHAPTER 4 TO TOOLKIT CONSTRUCTION SITE 1

The four research-based constructs selected in Chapter 3 for use as the foundation of a CBA need to be viewed from the perspective of school counseling contexts in which all students participate as part of the school counseling program. The motivation construct, for example, becomes relevant when applied to a specific context (e.g., student planning, college and career readiness, personal growth). It is essential in a CBA, therefore, that school counselors be able to describe what each construct means in terms of the relevant contexts discussed in this chapter.

As a result of completing Construction Site 1 tasks, you can expect to learn and do the following:

✓ Learn how to use relevant school counseling contexts as primary filters for designing, delivering and evaluating a CBA program.

✓ Determine which relevant contexts to incorporate into your CBA program.

Looking forward to working with you at the CBA Construction Site 1!

5 **Student Results**

Standards and Competencies

Scenario 1

Mira and Carlos, middle school counselors in Oceanview School District, were committed to demonstrating the results their program achieved for students. They developed a program for Grades 6 through 8 that taught students about the things they believed middle school students should know, including time management, learning style and organizational skills. Throughout the school year they collected data on the various lessons taught through their curriculum, and at the end of the year they presented their results to the administrators and faculty. Most of the audience was respectfully appreciative of the work the school counselors had done and the results they had achieved with their students. The next year the counselors implemented the same program for students and when they analyzed the data they had collected, they found that their results were not as impressive as the year before. They were puzzled and not sure what they had done wrong.

Scenario 2

Mira and Carlos had graduated from the same school counseling graduate program and were hired to work together in the middle school in Oceanview School District. They understood the construct-based approach to school counseling, and they set out to develop a program using schoolwide data to determine the needs of their students. They reviewed the construct-based student standards and developed competency statements that would demonstrate the knowledge and skills they sought to teach their students. Teaching lessons on the topics identified through this process, they collected data and presented their results to administrators and faculty at the last faculty meeting of the school year. They framed their presentation with the research that has determined the constructs they integrated in their program as important for students to learn. Then they explained why this approach would help students in all of their academic pursuits. The results were impressive, and their colleagues appreciative of the support the school counselors offered the students and faculty in helping all students achieve. The next school year Mira and Carlos followed the same process of reviewing data and determining the lessons that the students needed. Again, their results were impressive.

Reflections

Using the construct-based approach to school counseling helps school counselors provide a significant contribution to the education of their students. With well-established results statements, counselors understand how to provide challenging learning opportunities to help their students achieve excellence.

ACHIEVING EXCELLENCE

The book thus far has identified two primary filters (research-based constructs and relevant contexts) to articulate the conceptual foundation for a Construct-Based Approach (CBA) to school counseling programs. Four constructs (motivation, self-direction, self-knowledge, relationships) have been selected to focus our attention on specific areas of student development that can be significantly impacted by school counseling programs (see Chapter 3). In addition, five contexts in which students and school counselors interact were explored (Chapter 4). It is now time to explore how the constructs and contexts can be used to create a counseling-learning environment (CLE) in which students flourish and succeed.

The school counseling program is implemented to provide students with learning opportunities that help them achieve at their highest potential. What we are asking students to do as a result of participating in the school counseling program can be summed up in two words: Achieve Excellence. This chapter discusses the results we expect students to achieve in a construct-based, context-sensitive, counseling-learning environment.

COUNSELING-LEARNING ENVIRONMENT (CLE)

Education is all about learning. The notion of a "teaching-learning environment" highlights the inextricable relationship between teaching processes that help students learn and learning processes wherein students acquire the knowledge and develop the skills they need to succeed in school, work and life. The notion of a "counseling-learning environment" is introduced to identify aspects of the teaching-learning environment that are especially relevant to helping students achieve excellence through participation in the school counseling program.

Student excellence in a CLE is defined in terms of the results students are expected to achieve. Similarities and differences between teachers and school counselors were identified in Chapter 3. The definitions are repeated here in Table 5.1 as they help clarify the important role of school counselors in student development and specify the primary focus of counseling activities.

Table 5.1 Counselor and Teacher Roles

Shared Focus	Teachers	Counselors
While all good educators are invested in the holistic development of students, each attends to different facets of the educational experience which, when coordinated well, catalyze maximal learning and development.	Classroom teachers, for example, attend to the more obvious, observable and measureable aspects of achievement (e.g., facts, concepts and processes that reflect mastery of a particular area of knowledge) and enact effective instructional techniques that maximize students' opportunities to acquire knowledge and expertise.	In contrast, counselors help students develop the knowledge, skills, attitudes, beliefs and habits of mind that enable them to profit maximally from their instructional opportunities and experiences.

School counseling student results are defined in terms of helping students develop the knowledge, skills, attitudes, beliefs and habits of mind that lead to greater achievement and increased capacity for learning and success. A useful way to view these results is that we are helping students achieve excellence by providing opportunities for them to learn how to learn, plan for their future success, and cope with the many challenges of growing up and preparing to enter the post-secondary world.

TWO TYPES OF STUDENT RESULTS

A result can be defined as the end of a process and as a learning target. In a results-based approach, clearly articulated and measurable results define excellence. The results students are expected to achieve through participating in the school counseling program define student excellence in the counseling-learning environment. In short, the standard and competency statements reflect mastery-level competence or proficiency when they are achieved. A CBA school counseling program is designed and delivered with the intent to help students achieve and demonstrate excellence.

Figure 5.1 identifies two types of results, standards and competencies, which define student excellence along, and at the end of, the K–12 learning continuum. These statements form the central focus of the school counseling program: students achieving results (standards and competencies) that enable them to achieve and succeed at their highest potential in school, work and life.

As discussed in Chapter 2 ("A Simple Language Set"), standards are end results that students are expected to achieve by the time they graduate from high school. Student standards are end-of-the counseling-program results. Competencies are what students are expected to know and demonstrate at specified intervals along the K–12 learning continuum. Standard statements are informed by the four constructs. Competency statements are informed by the five contexts.

A CBA is grounded in a results-based approach to delivering school counseling programs wherein student results (outcomes), and how school counselors help students achieve them, are the central focus of the program. The counseling program is results based in that standard and competency statements are developed that define student excellence. The statements form the basis of the school counseling curriculum (Chapter 6) and provide the criteria by which student progress can be assessed (Chapter 7). The curriculum is the primary vehicle for offering students the opportunities to learn, apply what they are learning in authentic contexts, and demonstrate what they know and can do as a result of participating in the counseling program.

This chapter discusses the important role of standard and competency statements in a results-based CBA school counseling program.

A results-based counseling program "is designed to guarantee that all students acquire the competencies to become successful in school and to make a successful transition from school to higher education, to employment or to a combination of higher education and work. . . . The question to answer is: "How are students different as a result of the guidance program?" (Johnson et al., 2006, p. 7).

A results-based approach requires a clear definition of what students are expected to know and demonstrate as a result of the school counseling program. It also requires school counselors delivering high-quality learning opportunities in a variety of meaningful contexts. To say that students have

Figure 5.1 Two Types of Results

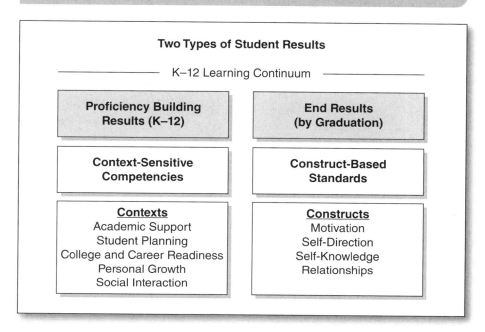

Two Types of Student Results

———————— K–12 Learning Continuum ————————

Proficiency Building Results (K–12)	**End Results (by Graduation)**
Context-Sensitive Competencies	**Construct-Based Standards**
Contexts Academic Support Student Planning College and Career Readiness Personal Growth Social Interaction	**Constructs** Motivation Self-Direction Self-Knowledge Relationships

achieved a result means that the students are competent, or proficient, in terms of the learning targets identified in the standard and competency statements. Achieving a result means that students have successfully demonstrated that relevant knowledge has been acquired and appropriate skills (successfully applying the knowledge in authentic contexts) have been developed.

The importance of student standards and competencies cannot be overemphasized. These statements represent the results we want students to achieve as a consequence of participating in the school counseling program. They represent the difference we are claiming the counseling program can make in students' lives and their ability to achieve and succeed.

It is this difference that school counselors can make in students' lives that is the primary focus of school counseling programs. Everything else school counselors do must be viewed as supporting the primary focus of making a difference in student lives and learning. Critical areas needed to support counselors' ability to make a difference include delivery of a rigorous school counseling curriculum, effective responsive services, contributing to school quality, ongoing professional development of highly qualified school counselors, counselor evaluation, and family and community engagement.

This is why a strong research base for CBA school counseling student standards is so important. School counselors need to know what they can and should do that has the greatest potential for, or has demonstrated the greatest impact in, helping students achieve and succeed.

CONSTRUCT-BASED STUDENT STANDARDS

As discussed in Chapter 2 ("A Simple Language Set"), standard statements focus on key areas of student learning and development, in this case the areas of motivation, self-direction, self-knowledge and relationships. Table 5.2

Table 5.2 CBA School Counseling Student Standards

Constructs	Standards
	[As a result of the school counseling program, students are expected to know and do the following by the time they graduate from high school.]
Motivation	Describe how their own motivation structure and patterns affect their current and future lives.
	Articulate a positive vision of their future that motivates present behavior.
	Consistently apply effective self-motivational techniques.
Self-Direction	Assess the factors responsible for their academic success and challenges and adjust their behavior accordingly.
	Demonstrate the self-direction, initiative and skills necessary for achievement and success.
	Maintain focus despite stress, anxiety and setbacks.
Self-Knowledge	Describe how their unique characteristics impact their current and future lives.
	Demonstrate how their skills and talents contribute to their success.
	Discuss how their values and interests inform their decisions and actions.
Relationships	Engage in collaborative and mutually beneficial relationships to promote individual and group success.
	Assess when they need help from others and seek assistance.
	Demonstrate fairness, respect and equity in relationships with others.

proposes twelve construct-based school counseling student standards (end of counseling program exit outcomes), with three standard statements for each of the four constructs.

All competency statements discussed in this book are aligned with these standards. An important question to answer is: What does it mean to say that a student has achieved the school counseling student standards? It means that students have demonstrated proficiency in terms of each of these of the standard and competency statements.

It must be remembered that standards are broad, general statements which, in and of themselves, are not measurable. For a standard to become measurable it must be contextualized, linked to authentic situations where it means something to counselors and students and is relevant to success in school and in the post-secondary world. Competency statements are the specific results that students should achieve in order to demonstrate their proficiency in completing critical tasks and progressing toward the school counseling student standards.

A VISION TO LIVE BY

It is important for school counselors to have a clear sense of what is expected of students who participate in their school counseling program. Figure 5.2 displays the four educational constructs and articulates a vision of student excellence by which we all can live.

Figure 5.2 A Vision to Live By

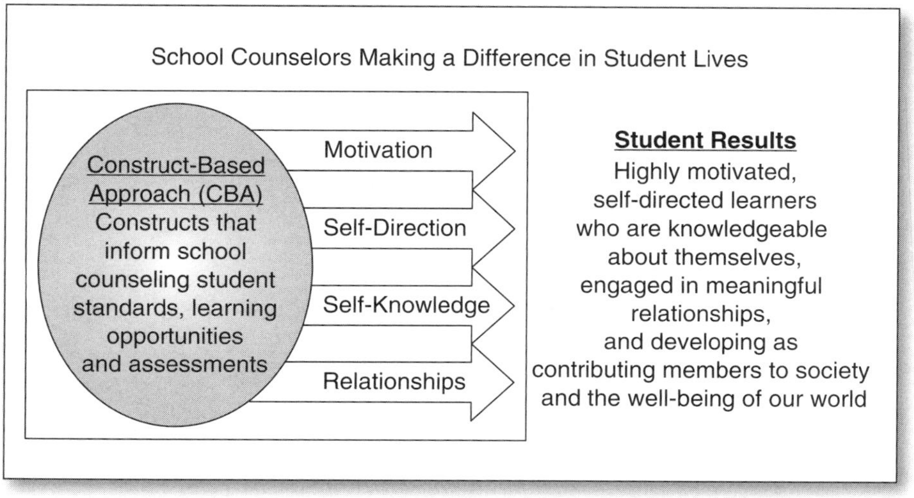

School Counselors Making a Difference in Student Lives

Construct-Based Approach (CBA) Constructs that inform school counseling student standards, learning opportunities and assessments

Motivation

Self-Direction

Self-Knowledge

Relationships

Student Results
Highly motivated, self-directed learners who are knowledgeable about themselves, engaged in meaningful relationships, and developing as contributing members to society and the well-being of our world

COMPETENCIES AS PROFICIENCY BUILDERS

Competency statements clarify the intent of the standard in measurable terms. Competencies are statements that describe requirements or conditions that must be met for a student to be deemed proficient. They provide more precise examples of evidence and proficiency that can be used to assess student progress at critical milestones along the learning continuum.

Johnson et al. (2006) offer the following definition of competencies and how they are used by counselors and other members of the school community:

> Competencies consist of developed proficiencies that are observable, transferable from a learning situation to a real-life situation, and directly aligned to a guidance goal. . . . Student support professionals, students, parents, and staff use competencies as indicators to measure whether students are moving toward the stated goals. (p. 21)

Competency statements serve a vital purpose in a results-based school counseling program. Understanding what they do and how to develop meaningful competency statements are central to fulfilling the role of a school counselor and delivering optimal opportunities for students to grow, develop and achieve the standards established for them. Competency statements allow school counselors to clearly define meaningful learning targets for students.

Learning targets convey to students the destination for the lesson—what to learn, how deeply to learn it and exactly how to demonstrate their new learning. The purpose and destination (expected results) for each learning opportunity is to provide valuable information to help students learn and achieve at higher levels. Without a precise description of where they are headed, too many students are "flying blind" (Moss, Brookhart, & Long, 2011, p. 66).

Competency statements are the specific learning targets students are expected to achieve along the K–12 learning continuum. It is critical that both school counselors and students grasp the meaning and significance of these statements and how achieving the results contribute to a capacity to learn.

WRITING MEANINGFUL COMPETENCY STATEMENTS

Well-constructed competency statements are essential to the successful implementation of a CBA. As noted earlier, competency statements clarify the intent of our construct-based student standards by adding specificity and helping to delineate what students should know and be able to do as a result of participating in the counseling program.

This section provides guidelines for writing meaningful competency statements, the achievement of which builds student proficiency. Sample competency statements are provided. Given the importance of competency statements, it is critical that school counselors understand both how to write meaningful statements and how to determine if the statements are challenging learning targets for students to achieve as they progress toward the standards.

Three important considerations when developing competency statements are identified in Figure 5.3 below. These considerations are intended to ensure that competency statements are challenging, measurable and effective learning targets that when met by students contributes to their achieving the school counseling standards.

Consideration 1: Competency Statements based on Constructs and Contexts

Competency statements in a construct-based, context-sensitive school counseling program define what students are expected to achieve in terms of each construct and context. A fully articulated school counseling program would include competency statements that specify learning targets for each construct (e.g., motivation) in terms of each context (e.g., academic support).

Figure 5.3   Three Considerations When Writing Competencies

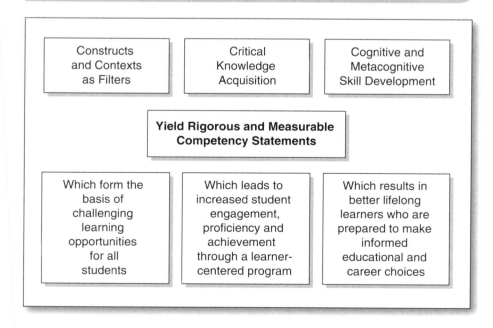

A starting point for developing meaningful competency statements is to ask what results we want students to achieve. For example, what results related to motivation do we expect students to achieve in terms of their academic achievement? Or, what results related to self-direction do we expect students to achieve in terms of planning for their future success? For any learning opportunity we are trying to develop, the first step is to ask what results we want students to achieve.

The essential processes that comprise each context (see Chapter 4: "Relevant Contexts for K–12 School Counseling Programs") are also important in developing meaningful competency statements. We can ask what results students are expected to achieve in each essential process. For example, in terms of student planning, competency statements can be developed regarding goal setting, creating action plans, monitoring progress and reflecting on one's progress.

Consideration 2: Knowledge

In order to demonstrate competence, or proficiency, in any learning effort requires essential knowledge related to the learning target that students must acquire to understand it, take action to achieve it, and monitor and self-assess their progress toward achievement. In developing competency statements, school counselors must consider any knowledge requirements that should be addressed in the competency statement.

The acquisition, retention and application of knowledge are central to the CBA learning process. Competency statements related to the acquisition of relevant knowledge should reflect what is important to know about the topic being taught. A simple example would be expecting students, after an anti-bullying intervention, to name three strategies they could use in a bullying situation. Or, an example of a longer-term competency would be expecting students to describe the basic steps in creating and maintaining a six-year individual learning plan. In both cases, knowledge needs to be acquired. Students need to be able to articulate that knowledge for themselves and communicate it to others. A key to developing competency statements is to determine what the relevant knowledge (e.g., ideas, concepts, vocabulary) is for the particular learning event.

Consideration 3: Cognitive and Metacognitive Learning Skills

Cognitive and metacognitive processes are essential to learning and, as such, are a critical focus for school counselors. Student skill development in school counseling programs is developed largely in terms of these two types of skills. Psychomotor skills are another set of skills that can serve as a source for writing meaningful competency statements, though this chapter will focus on cognitive and metacognitive skill development.

Conley (2013) defines metacognitive skills as "all learning processes and behaviors involving any degree of reflection, learning-strategy selection, and intentional mental processing that can result in a student's improved ability to learn" (para. 7).

What are cognitive and metacognitive skills, and what do they have to do with a CBA school counseling program? First, let's take a look at the characteristics of cognition and metacognition. "In science, cognition is the mental processing that includes the attention of working memory, comprehending and producing language, calculating, reasoning, problem solving, and decision making." Metacognition reflects a set of skills through which learners come to understand how they learn and to modify their own approaches to learning in order to become increasingly effective. Hacker, Dunlosky and Graesser (2009) indicated that metacognition consists of two related processes corresponding to knowledge of one's own cognition and regulation of one's own cognition. Knowledge of cognition consists of knowing the factors that influence one's learning and performance, knowing useful strategies for improving learning and performance, and knowing which strategy is most effective in a given situation. Regulation of cognition consists of planning and setting goals, monitoring the learning activity and evaluating one's own regulatory activities (assessing effectiveness of the strategies of that are employed).

In general terms, teachers are primarily concerned with cognitive processes while school counselors are primarily concerned with metacognitive processes, helping students to learn how to learn, plan for their future success and cope with the many barriers to their learning.

A FOCUS ON COGNITIVE SKILL DEVELOPMENT

It is important to consider cognitive skill development when constructing competency statements. If cognitive skills involve processes such as attention, memory, reasoning, problem solving and decision making, then we can ask what results students can be expected to achieve in terms of each of these processes. For example, we can write competency statements that can help students learn how to pay attention, or increase their capacity for remembering information, or learn the steps involved in making a decision or solving a problem.

An aspect of cognitive and metacognitive skill development concerns cognitive demand or depth of knowledge (DOK). In other words, how much mental processing is required to complete a task or achieve a competency statement (be able to demonstrate proficiency)?

Competency statements such as "Students will list three colleges they would like to attend" or "Students will name four test-taking strategies" do not require much mental processing. They simply require the ability to recall information that has been taught. A statement that reads "Students will complete and submit a college application" requires far more mental processing than simply recalling the name of three colleges. Likewise, a statement that reads "Students will describe the test-taking strategies they used and the impact of personally applying the strategies on the outcome of the test" requires far more mental processing that remembering the names of four strategies.

Depth of knowledge is referenced in No Child Left Behind (NCLB), which requires assessments to "measure the depth and breadth of the State academic content standards for any given grade level" (U.S. Department of Education, 2013, p. 12). It is defined as a "Mechanism to ensure that the intent of the standard and the level of student demonstration required by the standard matches the assessment items" (Maynus, n.d.; adapted from the model used by Norm Webb, University of Wisconsin, to align standards with assessments). Webb's Depth of Knowledge Model identified four levels of cognitive complexity that instruction and assessment should address. Table 5.3 displays Webb's four DOK levels (Webb, 2005, p. 12).

Although the DOK levels were developed for content areas—Reading, Language Arts, Mathematics, Science and Social Studies (N. L. Webb, Alt et al., 2005)—they are still informative in our efforts to determine how rigorous (mentally challenging) school counseling competency statements are for students participating in the CBA program. It is important to challenge students to achieve at their highest potential. Accomplishing this requires rigorous competency statements (learning targets) that challenge students to achieve excellence and demonstrate their proficiency in what they have learned.

Table 5.3   Webb's Depth of Knowledge Levels

Level	Name	Description
1	Recall	Recall of a fact, information or procedure.
2	Skill/ Development	Use information or conceptual knowledge, two or more steps, etc.
3	Strategic Thinking	Requires reasoning, developing a plan or sequence of steps, some complexity, more than one possible answer.
4	Extended Thinking	Requires an investigation, time to think and process multiple conditions of the problem.

A FOCUS ON METACOGNITIVE SKILL DEVELOPMENT

One way to identify metacognitive skills required for student success is to look at the type of "soft skills" discussed in Chapter 3 that are required in the SCANS Report, Partnership for 21st Century Skills and ACT. School counselors provide a necessary complement to the work of teachers because students need to learn to develop their metacognitive skills in order to profit maximally from a rigorous curriculum and effective instruction. Table 5.4 identifies important metacognitive skills identified in three national reform initiatives.

If these skills are required for success in the workplace, then competency statements can be developed for each of these skills. For example, a

Table 5.4 Metacognitive Skills are Critical to Student Success

SCANS	21st Century Skills	ACT
→ Listening to others → Participating effectively in groups → Understanding other's emotions → Dealing with cultural diversity → Managing oneself → Assuming responsibility → Managing one's own self-esteem → Decision making → Problem solving	→ Ability to maintain flexibility and adaptability → Ability to take initiative and be self-directed → Ability to manage difference and work collaboratively with others → Ability to accept responsibility and be accountable → Ability to lead others → Ability to act responsibly in the interests of the larger community	→ Motivation includes personal characteristics that help students succeed academically by focusing and maintaining energies on goal-directed activities. → Social engagement includes interpersonal factors that influence students' successful integration into their environment. → Self-regulation includes the thinking processes and emotional responses of students that govern how well they monitor, regulate, and control their behavior related to school and learning.

competency statement might read, "Students will demonstrate their ability to self-regulate their learning."

It is important for school counselors to consider metacognitive skill development when developing competency statements because of the significant impact of school counseling on student achievement and success. As Levin (2012) points out,

> To meet the economic, political, social, and personal demand for competency, much more is required of students and adults than just cognitive proficiencies as measured by test scores. Individuals must develop interpersonal skills that enable them to relate to others in many different societal situations. They must also develop the intrapersonal skills that include good judgment and strategies for meeting their own needs in effective ways. (p. 4)

Another example is provided by Durlak, Weissberg, Dymnicki, Taylor and Schellinger (2011), who conducted a meta-analysis of studies on social and emotional learning (SEL) programs in 213 K–12 schools involving 270,000 children aged 5 to 18. Levin (2012), reviewing the meta-analysis, concluded, "The effects of the interventions to improve social and emotional skills were comparable to or exceeded the results found in the literature for improving student achievement."

ROLE OF SCHOOL COUNSELORS

The core mission of K–12 school counseling programs is to help students succeed. To achieve success, students must learn. CBA school counseling programs can be designed to provide students with opportunities to learn how to learn. School counselors help students learn through the acquisition of critical knowledge about themselves, others and the world. Counselors help students develop skills that can help them achieve at higher levels and successfully pursue college and/or career pathways of their choice. School counselors help students understand that their attitudes, behaviors, values and habits of mind are critical to their future success. The key to helping students succeed begins with clearly defined and measurable competency statements, and communicating the importance of these results to future success and fulfillment.

Sample Competency Statements

Now that we have explored the rationale for using results statements (standards and competencies) to define student excellence in a counseling-learning environment, it will be helpful to look at some sample competency statements that are aligned with the proposed CBA school counseling student standards discussed earlier in this chapter. Table 5.5 provides sample competency statements at the elementary, middle and high school levels.

Table 5.5 Sample Competency Statements Aligned with Constructs

Construct	Standard (Students will:)	Level	Competency (Students will:)
Relationships	Demonstrate fairness, respect and equity in relationships with others.	Elementary	Describe a situation in which taking turns helped them.
Self-Knowledge	Demonstrate how their skills and talents contribute to their success.	Middle	Describe how knowing about themselves helped them reach their goals.
Motivation	Describe how their own motivation structure and patterns affect their current and future lives.	High	Identify their intrinsic and extrinsic motivations and how they impact their learning.

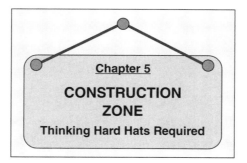

Chapter 5

CONSTRUCTION ZONE

Thinking Hard Hats Required

CONNECTING CHAPTER 5 TO TOOLKIT CONSTRUCTION SITE 1

Chapter 5 has focused on student results as articulated in CBA school counseling standard and competency statements. These are the learning targets we expect students to achieve as a result of participating in the school counseling program. It is the responsibility of school counselors to deliver a program that helps maximize students' potential for achieving these learning targets.

The CBA standard and competency statements, in and of themselves, have no real impact on student lives without a delivery vehicle for providing students with opportunities to learn what is expected of them, apply what they are learning in authentic contexts, and demonstrate their proficiency and achievement in what they have learned. The school counseling curriculum is the primary vehicle for delivering a CBA and will be discussed in Chapter 6.

As a result of completing Construction Site 1 tasks, you can expect to learn and do the following:

✓ Learn about the two primary types of student results in a CBA: standards and competencies and how they are used to define student excellence in school counseling programs.

✓ Explore a proposed set of CBA standards informed by research-based constructs and relevant school counseling contexts, and sample CBA competency statements that are measurable and aligned with the standards.

✓ Determine which constructs to incorporate into your CBA program.

Looking forward to working with you at the CBA Construction Site 1!

6 Role of Curriculum in a CBA

Scenario 1

Desert Springs School District hired Dr. Smart, its first Director of School Counseling, with the expectation that she would lead her department in the development of a comprehensive school counseling program, which was required by state policy. In an initial department meeting and through conversations and observations with her school counselors in their respective schools, Dr. Smart concluded that there was no documented curriculum in the district, nor was there any consistency in what was delivered in each school. She and the school counselors realized they needed to begin developing and documenting a program but weren't sure where to begin.

Scenario 2

Desert Springs School District hired Dr. Smart, its first Director of School Counseling, with the expectation that she would lead her department in the development of a comprehensive school counseling program, which was required by state policy. Dr. Smart had worked in a district that had used the Construct-Based Approach (CBA) to school counseling programs and was confident that she could apply the same approach in Desert Springs. In an initial department meeting and through conversations and observations with her school counselors in their respective schools, Dr. Smart was happy to learn that, while there was no documented curriculum, the school counselors were teaching lessons to all students and were open to a new and challenging approach. Dr. Smart shared the research that backed the CBA with her counselors and created several committees to begin the work.

Reflections

The CBA offers direction to the refinement or development of a school counseling program by showing critical areas that should be addressed by school counselors. A fully developed and documented curriculum is the primary vehicle for delivering content to all students. Special attention is paid to the fact that school counselors have a programmatic approach to delivering relevant content that will help students succeed in school and in life.

WHERE WE ARE IN THE CBA BUILDING PROCESS

Before delving into the role of curriculum, it might be helpful to review what we have put together so far in terms of building blocks for a Construct-Based Approach (CBA) to school counseling. Figure 6.1 identifies the five blocks.

We are currently in CBA Building Block (BB) 4. BB1 and BB2 have been established as primary filters for looking at students' learning and developmental needs. The review of research in Chapter 3 identified areas of student learning and development in which school counselors can have a significant impact by focusing on four research-based constructs: motivation, self-direction, self-knowledge and relationships.

Chapter 4, in order to make these constructs meaningful and relevant to school counselors and students, contextualized them in terms of five relevant contexts (common processes in which all students in a school counseling program participate). The contexts are student planning, academic support, college and career readiness, personal growth and social interaction.

The intersection of constructs and contexts (e.g., motivation in terms of personal growth, self-direction in terms of student planning, self-knowledge in terms of college and career readiness, relationships in terms of social interaction) provides a focus through which school counselors can determine what students will be expected to know, and demonstrate proficiency in, as a result of the CBA school counseling program.

Chapter 5 responded to the challenge of what students are expected to learn by proposing 12 CBA standard statements for student excellence, three standards for each construct (BB3). The statements serve as end results for the school counseling program: what students are expected to know and demonstrate by the time they graduate. In addition, sample CBA competency statements, aligned with the standard statements, were provided.

This brings us to our location at BB4, which contributes to a well-constructed CBA by delivering a challenging school counseling curriculum

Figure 6.1 CBA Building Blocks

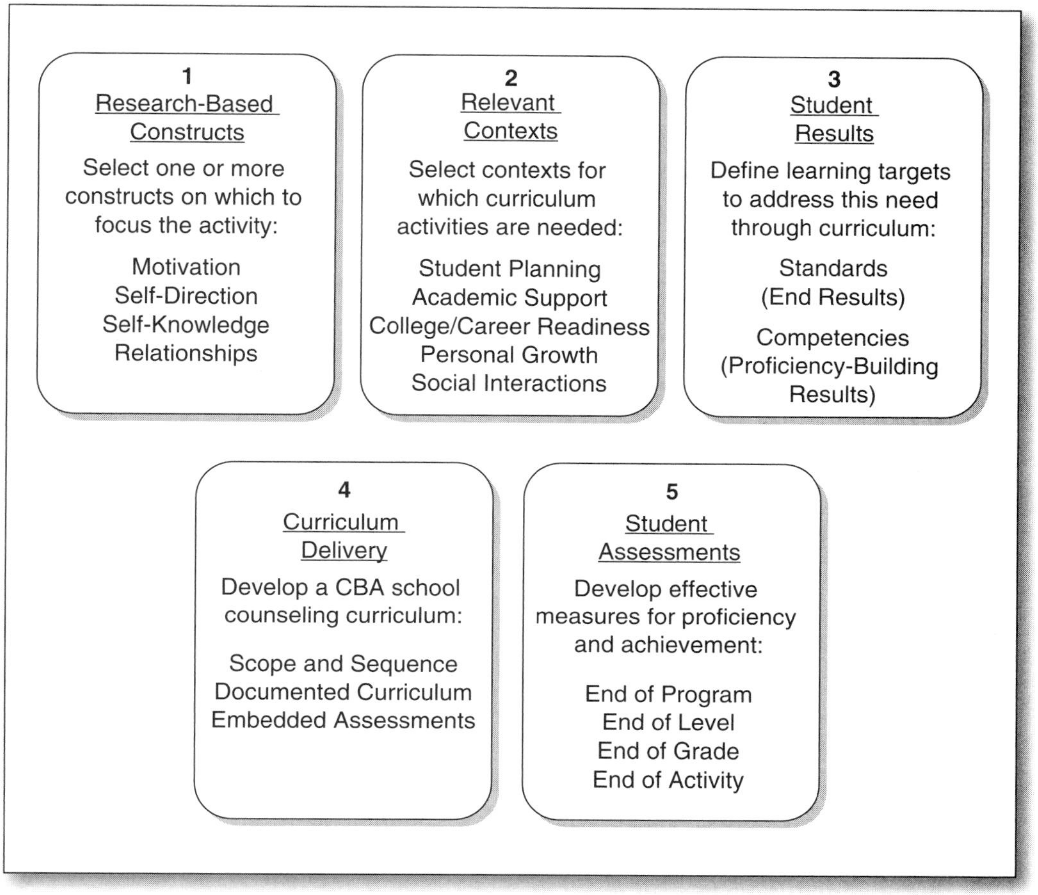

1
<u>Research-Based Constructs</u>

Select one or more constructs on which to focus the activity:

Motivation
Self-Direction
Self-Knowledge
Relationships

2
<u>Relevant Contexts</u>

Select contexts for which curriculum activities are needed:

Student Planning
Academic Support
College/Career Readiness
Personal Growth
Social Interactions

3
<u>Student Results</u>

Define learning targets to address this need through curriculum:

Standards
(End Results)

Competencies
(Proficiency-Building Results)

4
<u>Curriculum Delivery</u>

Develop a CBA school counseling curriculum:

Scope and Sequence
Documented Curriculum
Embedded Assessments

5
<u>Student Assessments</u>

Develop effective measures for proficiency and achievement:

End of Program
End of Level
End of Grade
End of Activity

that is based on CBA standard and competency statements, provides meaningful learning opportunities to help all students achieve what is expected of them, and allows for uniform assessment of all students' progress toward, and achievement of, the CBA standards.

By achieving these results (CBA standards and competencies defined for core school counseling curriculum activities), students will have demonstrated proficiency in what we have given them to learn. Students who successfully achieve the results embedded in the curriculum and other program offerings will have met the school counseling student standards. In terms of the vision to live by discussed in Chapter 5, students who achieve the school counseling standards will be highly motivated, self-directed learners who are knowledgeable about themselves, engaged in meaningful relationships and are contributing members to society.

Role of Curriculum in a CBA

The central focus of this chapter (Chapter 6) is on the role of the school counseling curriculum as the primary vehicle for delivering a standards-based school counseling program that provides equal learning opportunities to all students. The curriculum is the only aspect of a comprehensive school counseling program that fully supports an all-students agenda, that is, all students are provided equal opportunities to learn about the standards and work toward achieving them. In addition, the standards and competencies provide a context in which the progress, proficiency and achievement of all students can be uniformly measured.

A distinction is made between a core curriculum and the total curriculum offerings in a school counseling program. The term "core" is used to designate those curriculum activities that we feel every student should experience. The total curriculum can contain activities that are designed for subpopulations of students, but the core activities are intended to provide every student with equal and quality learning opportunities.

This chapter will explore the content of a core CBA curriculum (knowledge to be acquired, skills to be developed, attitudes/behaviors/habits of mind to be embraced) and how to organize the content as a developmentally appropriate sequence of learning opportunities leading to achievement of the CBA student standards.

The core CBA school counseling curriculum is intended for delivery to every student because of its importance as learning opportunities to student achievement and success in life.

Chapter 6, in conjunction with the *CBA Toolkit,* will guide you through the process of building a CBA curriculum, documenting it and evaluating the impact of delivering it. The student results discussed in Chapter 5 will be used in this chapter to illustrate how the results statements form the foundation and central focus of a CBA curriculum activity.

A sample K–12 CBA scope and sequence is provided in the Construction Zone at the end of this chapter, along with additional sample competency statements linked to CBA constructs and contexts. Finally, a sample documented CBA curriculum activity ("Send for Help") is provided in the Chapter 6 Construction Zone that addresses a critical student learning need that can be utilized by school counselors in their CBA program.

It is always difficult to imagine what completed products (e.g., scope and sequence, documented curriculum activity) really look like by simply reading an abstract description of them. Therefore, the scope and sequence and documented activity at the end of this chapter's Construction Zone are exemplars that can be used as models for your own CBA development work. The *CBA Toolkit* provides more examples and detailed instructions to assist in your efforts.

Chapter 7, which addresses BB5 (Student Assessments), focuses on assessing student proficiency and achievement, and using student data to serve students' individual learning needs while enhancing the quality of the counseling program and counselor practice.

Curriculum Delivery as a Preventive Approach

Every profession defines excellence for its members. A CBA focuses on student learning processes and how to help students become more productive learners. This is accomplished through the delivery of a learner-centered program that engages students and helps them along their developmental journey toward life in the post-secondary world and adulthood.

Research has demonstrated that school counseling programs have a positive impact on student development in terms of their academic and career success, and personal and social maturity (Carey & Dimmitt, 2012; Carey, Harrington, Hoffman, & Martin, 2012; Carey, Harrington, Martin, & Stevens, 2012). The CBA curriculum is designed as a preventive approach to addressing students' needs. It is delivered primarily through a core school counseling curriculum. It is an effort to deliver impactful learning opportunities early enough and frequently enough to make a difference in the development of students' thinking and behavior patterns.

ESSENTIAL CHARACTERISTICS OF A CBA CURRICULUM

We have identified the five building blocks of a CBA program. The task at hand is to take the constructs, contexts and student results (standards and competencies) developed in Chapters 3–5 and build a CBA school counseling curriculum consisting of core counseling activities designed to help all students achieve the CBA school counseling student standards.

It will be helpful to take a closer look at what characterizes a CBA curriculum because of its importance as the primary vehicle for successfully delivering a CBA program. Figure 6.2 displays eight defining characteristics.

These characteristics can be viewed as critical design principles for CBA curriculum activities, so when an activity is being developed and delivered, it should manifest these characteristics in order to provide meaningful learning opportunities to students. Each characteristic is discussed below.

Construct Based

The curriculum focuses on areas in which research has demonstrated that school counselors potentially can have the greatest impact. Four research-based constructs have been selected for the CBA: motivation, self-direction, self-knowledge and relationships. Three standard statements

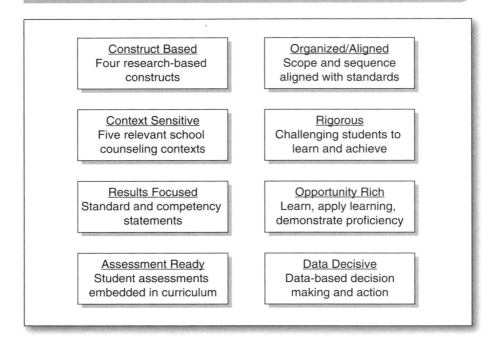

Figure 6.2 CBA Curriculum Characteristics

Construct Based Four research-based constructs	**Organized/Aligned** Scope and sequence aligned with standards
Context Sensitive Five relevant school counseling contexts	**Rigorous** Challenging students to learn and achieve
Results Focused Standard and competency statements	**Opportunity Rich** Learn, apply learning, demonstrate proficiency
Assessment Ready Student assessments embedded in curriculum	**Data Decisive** Data-based decision making and action

were suggested for each construct in Chapter 5. The standard statements represent what school counselors hope students will exhibit by the time they graduate. Competency statements add specificity and measurability along the K–12 learning continuum in terms of what knowledge, skills and behaviors students need to learn and demonstrate to meet the CBA student standards.

The school counseling curriculum, like content-area curricula, is standards based and has content to deliver. Curriculum content (knowledge, skills, attitudes/behaviors) is designed to provide students with meaningful opportunities to learn, apply their learning and demonstrate their proficiency. Core curriculum activities are intended for all students and are generally delivered in whole class environments. Curriculum can also be delivered in small group settings and be the basis of strategies to help students with knowledge and skill deficiencies to improve their learning processes and results.

Context Sensitive

For standard statements to become measurable, they must be contextualized. For example, one of the proposed standard statements for the self-direction construct is "Students will demonstrate the self-direction, initiative and skills necessary for achievement and success." It is obvious that this statement in and of itself is not measurable without further detail. Competency statements provide the specificity needed to assess student progress toward standards along the K–12 learning continuum. Competencies are proficiency-building results. Achieving the competencies set for the activity enables students to increase their level of proficiency as they progress toward the student standards with which the competencies are aligned.

It is not necessarily the intent of a competency statement to introduce a learning target to students and have them become proficient in the same session. For example, a lesson on bullying could take multiple sessions, or a student planning process can take an entire school year. Rather, a single curriculum activity plus related curriculum and program activities collectively are used to build proficiency until students have met or exceeded the competency and standard statements.

Competency statements are articulated in terms of relevant contexts. Five contexts have been suggested: student planning (individual learning plans), academic support, college and career readiness, personal growth and social interaction. These contexts provide the detail that is required to set benchmarks for student performance throughout their involvement with the school counseling program.

The five contexts are each composed of essential processes (see Chapter 4) that students must successfully navigate to fully benefit from their school experience. Counselors help students to become proficient in processes that are going to help them succeed academically, select and explore career pathways, and effectively manage their personal and social development. CBA competency statements represent the knowledge, skill and behavior requirements that are necessary to help students achieve the CBA student standards.

Results Focused

A discussion about the best ways to provide optimal learning opportunities to students begins with a discussion of the results we want students to achieve and what we expect them to learn and accomplish through participation in a CBA school counseling program. Focusing on results enables school counselors to determine at the onset the difference they expect to see in students' thinking and behavioral patterns as a result of their learning. Once the expected student outcomes have been established, it is then possible to systematically develop and deliver the processes needed for students to achieve the results.

Results based means that the counseling program is designed to help students achieve the outcomes (standards and competencies) expected of them. Students are expected to achieve two types of results as a consequence of participating in the school counseling program. The first is a standard—an end result that they are expected to achieve by the time they graduate from high school. The second is a competency—a proficiency-building result that students are expected to achieve all along the K–12 learning continuum.

The curriculum is the primary delivery vehicle for helping all students work toward and achieve the school counseling student standards. The curriculum is an integrated set of learning opportunities that helps students acquire relevant knowledge, develop skills appropriate to their educational and vocational pathways, and embrace those attitudes and behaviors that lead to success.

All curriculum activities use competency statements to identify what students should know and do as a result of the activity. The curriculum is designed to help students learn what is expected of them, how to apply their knowledge to authentic situations and how to demonstrate their proficiency in terms of the competency statements.

Results based means starting out with a clear sense of the outcomes to be achieved. The curriculum is aligned with the standards and provides a roadmap for getting to the destination (demonstration of proficiency/competence in terms of school counseling standard and competency statements).

The counseling curriculum requires clearly articulated standards and competencies that define what students are expected to achieve. They are based on knowledge and skill requirements for future success. The statement(s) used to articulate the standards focus on critical aspects of student development that counseling professionals want to impact.

Organized and Aligned

Counseling curriculum activities, organized in a developmentally appropriate scope and sequence, must be aligned with relevant standards and competency statements. The student assessments embedded in the school counseling curriculum activities must be aligned with the content taught. For example, in a curriculum activity on bullying, assessments should focus on assessing students' knowledge and skills that were taught in the class.

The purpose of aligning the curriculum activities with the standards and competencies is to ensure that students are provided with opportunities to achieve the standards. When an activity is aligned with one or more standards, it means that the activity is capable of helping students progress toward the stated competencies for the activity in the short term and the standards as a long-term outcome.

Rigorous

The curriculum must be rigorous. It must challenge students to exercise their full potential for learning. It must help students advance as far as possible toward achieving entry-level knowledge and skills for the post-secondary world of further education, training and work. The curriculum is an integrated set of learning opportunities in which students and counselors interact to achieve specific results (learning outcomes). It is based on clearly defined results—outcomes students are expected to achieve through participation in the counseling program.

Core school counseling curriculum activities are designed specifi-cally to provide students with optimal and multiple opportunities to learn and achieve. The CBA's learner-centered curriculum helps establish a counseling-learning environment that engages students and personalizes their learning experience.

The CBA's school counseling curriculum is challenging and focuses students' attention on how they learn, how well they are progressing in their learning and what they can do to improve. Grounding the curriculum in the four constructs enables students to learn about what motivates them, what makes them think and behave the way they do, or gives them a sense of belonging and fulfillment.

Students, in order to succeed, need to be concerned about goal setting and planning for their future. Students need to be effective in reflecting on their experience and making adjustments in order to improve. A rigorous curriculum provides an environment for challenging students to take charge of their lives and ownership of their learning.

Opportunity Rich

The school counseling curriculum activities are aligned with the construct-based student standards and competencies. A rigorous (challenging) curriculum ensures that students are provided opportunities to learn, apply and demon-strate proficiency in what they are being taught.

A CBA provides students with opportunities to learn what they are being taught, multiple opportunities to practice their learning by applying it in authentic contexts, and opportunities to show others what they know and can do. It is also an opportunity to get immediate and ongoing feedback on how well they have performed in demonstrating their proficiency.

Assessment processes and instruments to determine student progress toward stated results are defined for, and embedded in, each curriculum activity. The counseling curriculum is viewed as the primary delivery system for standards-based activities because it is a defined set of core activities (scope and sequence) that is delivered to all students and is most capable of uniform assessment of student progress toward the student standards. It is important to note that students also work toward many of the defined com-petencies outside of the planned counseling program.

Data Decisive

A required component in every curriculum activity is one or more competency statements (student learning targets) that define what students are expected to know and do as a result of the activity. Another required component is embedded assessments (processes and instruments for determining student progress toward the activity's competency statements). It is not necessary to use embedded assessments every time the activity is delivered to students. However, in a CBA, it is important that the ability to assess student progress in meaningful ways in each activity be developed and documented. This ensures that assessments are available to determine what and how well students are learning in relation to what is stated in the competency statements. See Chapter 7 ("Assessing Student Proficiency and Achievement in a CBA") for a more detailed discussion regarding embedded assessments in CBA school counseling curriculum activities.

Results from embedded assessment can be reported to demonstrate progress in program implementation. The primary beneficiaries of embedded assessment results are students and counselors. Others may also benefit from the results (e.g., parents, teachers, other support team personnel).

The data gathered from assessments embedded in curriculum activities, plus data from other sources (student information system, interventions such as Response to Intervention [RTI]), are used to make data-based decisions regarding students' needs and strategies/interventions that support helping students fulfill their needs. Data are critical to the success of a CBA school counseling program and to providing compelling evidence of the value of K–12 school counselors on student achievement, school improvement and program quality.

PRINCIPLES FOR LEARNER-CENTERED SCHOOL COMMUNITIES

The American Psychological Association (APA, 1997) published 14 psychological principles of learning. These principles significantly informed the design of the CBA described by defining the essential characteristics of sustainable, learner-centered school communities.

These 14 principles focus on learners and the learning process. They reflect internal psychological factors influencing self-regulated learning. The principles also consider external factors, such as environment or context that interact with the internal factors. These principles emphasize the active and reflective nature of learning and learners. From this perspective, educational practice will be most likely to improve when the educational system is redesigned with the primary focus on the learner (APA, 1997).

The alignment of construct-based student standards, curriculum activities and student assessments enables a CBA to establish a counseling-learning environment that is supportive of each student's personal development and their development as social beings.

The 14 principles are distributed among four categories: a) cognitive and metacognitive factors, b) motivational and affective factors, c) developmental and social factors, and d) individual differences factors. The applications of these principles to CBA-based school counseling are described below:

1. Nature of the learning process

School counselors should know about student learning processes and how to effectively identify and respond to students' needs. The first requirement is to establish a counseling-learning environment that is both meaningful for students (they find meaning there) and to provide learning opportunities that maximize students' potential to construct meaning in ways that best serve their goals and aspirations.

Based on this principle, a CBA needs to establish an environment in which students can make their construction of meaning an intentional process. A big part of the meaning we want students to construct centers on the construct-based results (standards and competencies). These are the learning targets established for student achievement and performance. In addition to standards of student excellence, a CBA provides a learner-centered curriculum based on the student standards.

A CBA is fully aligned with these characteristics of a successful learner: "active, goal-directed, self-regulating, and assume personal responsibility for contributing to their own learning" (APA, 1997).

2. Goals of the learning process

For these meaningful, coherent representations to develop, students must "generate and pursue personally relevant goals" (APA, 1997).

These representations of knowledge inform how we look at ourselves and our place in the world. It is important for school counselors, using a CBA, to recognize that this is a process that occurs over time and that the curriculum provides students with developmentally appropriate learning opportunities to construct self-knowledge based on information and one's experiences.

3. Construction of knowledge

Students are constantly bombarded by new information that needs to be processed and applied in decision-making processes (APA, 1997). A CBA is particularly interested in the impact of new knowledge on a student's self-knowledge and self-concept.

4. Strategic thinking

Strategic thinking looks to the future and seeks to determine the results one hopes to accomplish and how they will be achieved (APA, 1997). A CBA teaches students the knowledge and skills they need to do well in school and in life. Evidence-based practices should be used whenever possible.

"Learning outcomes can be enhanced if educators assist learners in developing, applying, and assessing their strategic learning skills" (APA, 1997). A theme of this book has been that school counselors provide students with metacognitive skill development. To accomplish this, school counselors help students reflect on their learning processes and find ways to improve them.

5. Thinking about thinking

This is captured succinctly in "Successful learners can reflect on how they think and learn, set reasonable learning or performance goals, select potentially appropriate learning strategies or methods, and monitor their progress toward these goals" (APA, 1997).

Successful learners are adaptive, seeking alternative ways to achieve their goals, when needed. "Instructional methods that focus on helping learners develop this higher order (metacognitive) strategies can enhance student learning and personal responsibility for learning" (APA, 1997).

6. Context of learning

Contexts are important because they provide information about students that enables school counselors to more fully understand the influences that shape a student's learning style and processes. Culture, for example, can influence students' "motivation, orientation toward learning, and ways of thinking" (APA, 1997). A lack of understanding diminishes the effectiveness of student-counselor interactions.

Instructional practices play an especially important role in that these are the strategies employed in student-counselor interactions. The strategies that are applied, therefore, should have the capacity to help students progress toward the construct-based school counseling student standards. The primary strategies incorporated in a construct-based school counseling core curriculum use the constructs as a primary filter in establishing student need and determining appropriate interventions.

7. Motivational and emotional influences on learning

Motivation is a key to understanding learning. As one of the foundational components of a CBA, it is expected that helping students increase their motivation will improve their capacity to learn and achieve. Student beliefs about "themselves as learners and the nature of learning have a marked influence on motivation. Motivational and emotional factors also influence both the quality of thinking and information processing as well as an individual's motivation to learn" (APA, 1997). Positive emotions can generally enhance learning and performance while negative emotions "generally detract from motivation, interfere with learning, and contribute to low performance" (APA, 1997).

8. Intrinsic motivation to learn

This principle brings together the notions of novelty, difficulty, relevance, personal choice and control (APA, 1997). All these factors heavily influence students' intrinsic motivation to learn. All address critical factors in students' personal growth. All are aligned with the functions of motivation, self-direction, self-knowledge and relationships. The principle identifies specific properties of a counseling-learning environment: It must be novel enough to attract and hold students' interests. The environment must be challenging. The learning experience will not be as relevant and meaningful to the learner unless it has a level of difficulty that must be achieved. Everyone likes to have choices they can make, be free to make them and have at least some control in the situations to which the choices are relevant.

A CBA provides learning opportunities that are personally relevant and meaningful to students, linked to real-life situations students will confront and are requisite to future success in school, life and work and are "appropriate in complexity and difficulty to the learners' abilities, and on which they believe they can succeed" (APA, 1997).

9. Effects of motivation on effort

Effort, the work required to complete a task or program, can indicate a student's motivation to learn (APA, 1997). We all want students to be motivated to learn. A CBA helps ensure that students are committed to the learning process and are committed to reaching their learning targets by exploring how they learn. Counselors guide students in this process of understanding the effort required and completing it. This is especially evident in student planning as the question of how much effort is required and how well are students exerting that effort is a constant focus on the planning process. Many strategies are used, including "purposeful learning activities, guided by practices that enhance positive emotions and intrinsic motivation to learn, and methods that increase learners' perceptions that a task is interesting and personally relevant" (APA, 1997).

10. Developmental influences on learning

Individual students differ in how they learn. No one approach is going to fulfill the learning needs of every student (APA, 1997). The CBA utilizes a differentiated approach to curriculum delivery. Competency statements are developmentally appropriate, and the core counseling activities that help students achieve those results are organized into a scope and sequence of activities that instill in students appropriate thinking and behavior patterns.

11. Social influences on learning

The "relationships" construct is particularly relevant to this principle. Collaboration with others in performing instructional tasks can enhance a student's learning potential (APA, 1997). A CBA encourages collaboration and teamwork as a primary strategy for teaching students about the workplace and what employers requirement in terms of knowledge, skills and performance at work.

Helping student learn how to interact socially and as a team player is a major part of the counselor's role. "Quality personal relationships that provide stability, trust, and caring can increase learners' sense of belonging, self-respect and self-acceptance, and provide a positive climate for learning" (APA, 1997). Family and positive learning climate are also important influences that are considered when thinking about student learning and how to harness the relationships in ways that will help students grow and achieve.

12. Individual differences in learning

A CBA uses differentiated instruction to help address individual student needs. For a CBA to be learner centered, it needs to be exactly that: centered on the learner. The programmatic approach of a school counseling program addresses the needs of all students (the core curriculum delivered to everyone) and the needs of targeted subpopulations and that of individual students.

13. Learning and diversity

"When learners perceive that their individual differences in abilities, backgrounds, cultures, and experiences are valued, respected, and accommodated in learning tasks and contexts, levels of motivation and achievement are enhanced" (APA, 1997). A CBA encourages students to recognize and respect differences.

14. Standards and assessment

The CBA described in this book proposed a set of 12 standards (exit outcomes), three standards each for the constructs of motivation, self-direction, self-knowledge and relationships.

"Self-assessments of learning progress can also improve students self-appraisal skills and enhance motivation and self-directed learning" (APA, 1997). One of the key components in individual learning plans is self-reflection. Students reflect on the goals they establish in the beginning of the school year, the steps they took to work toward their goals, their accomplishments and challenges. Students make determinations about what to do with their lives in the short and long term based on their reflections.

RESULTS-BASED CBA CURRICULUM IN A NUTSHELL

As evidenced in the discussion above, a CBA school counseling curriculum plays a vital role in delivering a comprehensive program and establishing a learner-centered school counseling environment conducive to all students achieving at higher levels. Figure 6.3 shows the essential steps in delivering a results-based CBA school counseling curriculum. See the scope and sequence and documented curriculum activity exemplars in the Construction Zone below.

Figure 6.3 Delivering a Results-Based Curriculum to All Students

Standard and Competency Statements	Curriculum activities are based on the standard and competency statements and are delivered to help students achieve the counseling standards
Curriculum Scope and Sequence	Core curriculum activities are organized in a developmentally appropriate scope and sequence
Documented Activities	Curriculum activities in the scope and sequence are documented with clearly defined student outcomes and embedded assessments
Curriculum Delivery	Challenging learning opportunities are delivered to students to help them progress toward and achieve the school counseling standards
Student Assessment	Student progress toward the standard is assessed periodically: End of Program, End of Level, End of Grade, End of Activity
Student Results Reporting	Data on student results is shared with students and families, displayed on the report card and reported to relevant constituencies in the school community

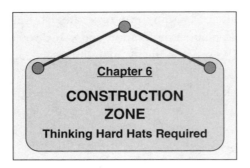

CONNECTING CHAPTER 6 TO TOOLKIT CONSTRUCTION SITE 2

The CBA curriculum is the primary vehicle for delivering a construct-based approach to school counseling. It is built upon CBA standards and competencies that are informed by research-based constructs and relevant school counseling contexts. Competency statements define what knowledge and skills students are expected to learn and successfully apply in a variety of situations.

The curriculum provides students with opportunities to learn how to learn, plan for their future success and demonstrate their proficiency in what they have been asked to learn. It is a planned set of learning opportunities that can be delivered systematically to all students, help ensure equity and provide a context in which student progress toward school counseling standards can be assessed. Construction Site 2 will help you develop, deliver and assess the impact of your CBA school counseling curriculum.

As a result of completing Construction Site 2 tasks, you can expect to learn and do the following:

✓ Learn how to produce a developmentally appropriate scope and sequence of CBA core curriculum activities.

✓ Learn how to develop and document core CBA curriculum activities.

✓ Learn how to embed assessments in CBA curriculum activities and use the data to guide students' learning processes.

✓ Learn how to develop your own meaningful competency statements and use them as the learning targets for the CBA school counseling curriculum.

✓ Develop a plan for producing a "Curriculum Framework for School Counseling" that documents the programmatic nature of the school counseling program.

Looking forward to working with you at Toolkit Construction Site 2!

EXAMPLE 6-A

CBA Scope and Sequence

CBA Sample Elementary School Counseling Scope and Sequence

Activity names are followed by initials reflecting the construct that the activity teaches. Some activities could teach different constructs depending on how the unit is designed or the timing of the activity. For example, a career exploration and vocational planning activity in 8th grade is primarily motivational, while in the 12th grade is a pragmatic self-knowledge activity or self-direction activity.

M = Motivation, SK = Self-Knowledge, SD = Self-Direction, R = Relationships

Grades K–1	Grades 2–3	Grades 4–5
→ Feelings (SK) → Empathy (R) → Listening (SD) → Calming Down Strategies (SD) → Fairness (R) → Problem-Solving Strategies (SD) → Career Awareness (M) → Anger Management (SD) → Bully Awareness (R) → Respectful Behavior (R) → Personal Space (SD)	→ Goal Setting (M) → Conflicting Feelings (SK) → Recognizing Different Feeling (SK) → Listening and Expressing (SD) → Perceptions and Intentions (SD) → Calming Down Strategies (SD) → Stress Management (SD) → Peer Pressure (R) → Problem-Solving Strategies (SD) → Anger Management (SD) → Bully Prevention (R) → Career Interest Inventory (SK)	→ Test-Taking Strategies (SD) → Organizational Skills (SD) → Goal Setting (M) → Progress Monitoring (M) → Reflection (SD) → Bullying: Rumors and Gossip (R) → Learning Styles (SK) → Career Exploration (M) → Peer Pressure (R) → Recognizing and Accepting Differences (R) → Connections/Team Building (R) → Coping Skills (SD)

CBA Sample Middle School Counseling Scope and Sequence

Activity names are followed by initials reflecting the construct that the activity teaches. Some activities could teach different constructs depending on how the unit is designed or the timing of the activity. For example, a career exploration and vocational planning activity in 8th grade is primarily motivational, while in the 12th grade it is a pragmatic self-knowledge activity or self-direction activity.

M = Motivation, SK = Self-Knowledge, SD = Self-Direction, R = Relationships

Grade 6	Grade 7	Grade 8
→ Academic and Personal Planning (Goal Setting) (M) → Organizational Skills, Use of Agenda (SD) → Peer Pressure (R) → Study Skills (SD) → Goal Self-Reflection and Planning (M) → Career Interest Inventory (SK) → Personal Strengths and Challenges (SK) → Respect for Self and Others (R)	→ Academic and Personal Planning (Goal Setting) (M) → Organizational Skills, Use of Agenda (SD) → Time Management (SD) → Anti-Bullying (R) → Study Skills Part 1 (SD) → Peer Mediation Training (R) → Learning Style Inventory (SK) → Friendship (R) → Academic and Personal Plan Review (SK) → Test-Taking Strategies (SD) → Goal Self-Reflection and Planning (M) → Career Exploration (M)	→ Academic and Personal Planning (Goal Setting) (M) → Homework, Use of Agenda (SD) → Time Management (SD) → Anti-Bullying (R) → Study Skills Part 2 (SD) → Peer Mediation Training (R) → High School Academic Planning (SK) → Getting Along/ Peer Relations (R) → Academic and Personal Plan Review (M) → Test-Taking Strategies (SD) → Goal Self-Reflection and Planning (M) → Career Exploration, Academic Requirements (SK) → Personality Styles (SK)

CBA Sample High School Counseling Scope and Sequence

Activity names are followed by initials reflecting the construct that the activity teaches. Some activities could teach different constructs depending on how the unit is designed or the timing of the activity. For example, a career exploration and vocational planning activity in 8th grade is primarily motivational, while in the 12th grade is a pragmatic self-knowledge activity or self-direction activity.

M = Motivation, SK = Self-Knowledge, SD = Self-Direction, R = Relationships

Grade 9	Grade 10	Grade 11	Grade 12
→ Academic and Personal Goal Setting (M) → Succeeding in High School (M) → Learning Styles (SK) → Basic Skills (SK) → Work Values (SK) → How You See Yourself (SK) → Career Search (M) → Interest Inventory (SK) → Interest Profiler (SK)	→ Academic and Personal Goal Setting (M) → Personality/ Temperament Style (SK) → Picture Yourself in the Future (M) → Personal Management Style (SK) → Self-Advocacy (SD) → Money Matters (SK) → Junior Year Plan (M) → Career Clusters Transferable Skills (M)	→ Academic and Personal Goal Setting (M) → Learning Styles (SK) → Academic Audit (transcript) (SK) → Post-Secondary Options (SK) → Test-Taking Skills (SD) → Decision Making (SD) → Senior Year and Beyond (SK) → Career Planning (M) → Post-Secondary Search (SK)	→ Academic and Personal Goal Setting (M) → Graduation Requirement Review/ Audit (SK) → Job-Seeking (SD) → Employability Skills (SD) → Transition to Post-Secondary (SK) → Picture Yourself in the Future (M) → Post-Secondary Search (SK) → Resume Writing (SD)

EXAMPLE 6-B

Documented CBA Curriculum Activity: "Send for Help"

Students: All students in Grades 6–8.

Sessions: Multiple sessions as determined by counselor and teacher.

CBA Counseling Standards Addressed
(Standards are listed at end of this activity)

Motivation			Self-Direction			Self-Knowledge			Relationships		
M1	M2	M3	SD1	SD2	SD3	SK1	SK2	SK3	R1	R2	R3

Competency Statements

Competency Statements (As a result of participating in this activity, students will:)		Opportunities We Provide Students to Demonstrate Progress toward Results	Assessments Used with Each Competency Statement
1	Identify and invite experts to help expand their knowledge and develop their skills.	Complete a written response (worksheet with guiding questions) on documenting the steps.	Student Worksheet
2	Effectively communicate to experts their problems and the kind of assistance they need.	Complete a written response (worksheet with guiding questions) on documenting the steps.	Student Worksheet
3	Demonstrate what they learn from experts to improve their learning.	Describe how they applied what they learned in their school work and/or personal lives (e.g., oral report, journal entry, essay).	Criteria Checklist/ Rubric

Preparations

Complete the following preparations prior to introducing the activity to students:

– Collaborate with a content area teacher to deliver this activity, having students identify something in the content area that they, as a class, are having trouble learning.

– Contact invited experts in advance to let them know the invitation is coming, what is expected of them and how they can best help your students. Recommend that they describe and/or demonstrate what they do (e.g., steps involved in successfully doing their job, special techniques they use, examples of how they achieve excellence). Ask them to include hands-on opportunities for students, and provide them with feedback on their performance.

– Develop a list of key concepts and vocabulary, with definitions, to introduce to your students, including:

+ Expert—an individual who has knowledge about, or experience in, areas in which the students need help.

+ Expert Advice—the information and tools an "expert" shares with others about the best way to get things accomplished.

Resources

The following resources are used in this activity.

– "Send for Help" Worksheet.

– Flip charts/boards and markers for brainstorming activities.

– Session Activities

Note: This activity is best delivered by a counselor collaborating with a content area teacher, enabling the students to select an area of learning in which they need help. Some of the action steps are best completed using a full class period (e.g., visit to class by expert), and others can be completed as a class segment by the counselor and teacher. You should decide how many sessions you will need and what action steps are included in each session.

Session 1

Step	Who	Action Steps
1	Counselor & Teacher	Introduce the "Send for Help" activity to your students, including the concepts/vocabulary and the "Send for Help" Worksheet.
2	Students	Brainstorm what they do when they need help with their learning, and document their ideas.

(Continued)

(Continued)

Step	Who	Action Steps
3	Students	Identify (as a class) something they are learning for which they need help (to acquire/expand their knowledge or develop their skills).
4	Students	Brainstorm how they might go about finding an "expert" to help them, and then select an expert to contact and ask for help.
5	Students	Achieve consensus on what information the expert needs from them in order to prepare for the visit (e.g., concise statement of problem area for which they need help, what is expected of the expert, when and where help is needed). The information should be documented and included in the students' invitation.
6	Students	Determine the best method for making the contact (e.g., phone call, letter, e-mail) and prepare the invitation asking the expert to visit the class and help them solve their problem of too little information and not enough skill.
7	Students	Deliver the invitation to the expert.

Session 2

Step	Who	Action Steps
1	Students	Brainstorm how to capture and organize what the expert will share (e.g., by phrasing and asking relevant questions, documenting what the expert is saying, participating in hands-on activities).
2	Students	Select a student or group of students to host the invited guest, and rehearse the role and responsibilities of being a host.

Session 3

Step	Who	Action Steps
1	Students	Meet with the expert.

Step	Who	Action Steps
		Session 4
1	Counselor	Arrange opportunities for students to hold follow-up discussions, apply the knowledge they learned to the area for which they needed help and work on developing those skills the expert considers important to success.
2	Students	Send a thank-you note, including a description of the most important lessons the class learned from the expert's visit.
3	Students	Complete the "Send for Help" Worksheet and maintain a copy in their portfolio.
4	Counselor & Teacher	Review the completed "Send for Help" Worksheets to assess student progress toward stated results for this activity. Provide whole class and individual feedback, as appropriate.

"Send for Help" Worksheet

This worksheet is to document the steps you would take to get an expert to help you, and to identify the most important lessons you learned when the expert visited your school. Complete all items and keep this worksheet with your portfolio.

Steps Prior to the Visit

 – What steps will I take to identify and contact an expert for help?

 – What kind of information does the expert need from me before visiting the school?

 – How will I get ready for an expert to visit my class?

 – How will I document what the expert says is important for me to know and be able to do?

Steps Following the Visit

 – Name the most important lessons I learned from the expert who visited my class.

 – Give examples of how I applied these lessons to help me learn better.

Expert's Criteria Checklist/Rubric

- Record whether or not the student completed the steps successfully by indicating "Yes" or "No" in the "Completed or Not" column.

- Record your assessment of how well a student completed each step (on a scale of 1–5).

Complete the following rubric for each student.

Student Name _____ Date _____

1 = Strongly Disagree; 2 = Disagree; 3 = Neither Agree nor Disagree; 4 = Agree; 5 = Strongly Agree

		Completed or Not (Y/N)	1	2	3	4	5
Before the Session	What steps will I take to identify and contact an expert for help?						
	What kind of information does the expert need from me before visiting the school?						
	How will I get ready for an expert to visit my class?						
During the Session	How will I document what the expert says is important for me to know and be able to do?						
After the Session	Name the most important lessons I learned from the expert who visited my class.						
	Give examples of how I applied these lessons to help me learn better.						

EXAMPLE 6-C

CBA Student Standards

Constructs	Standards
	[As a result of the school counseling program, students are expected to know and demonstrate the following by the time they graduate from high school.]
Motivation	Describe how their own motivation structure and patterns affect their current and future lives.
	Articulate a positive vision of their future that motivates present behavior.
	Consistently apply effective self-motivational techniques.
Self-Direction	Assess the factors responsible for their academic success and challenges, and adjust their behavior accordingly.
	Demonstrate the self-direction, initiative, and skills necessary for achievement and success.
	Maintain focus despite stress, anxiety and setbacks.
Self-Knowledge	Describe how their unique characteristics impact their current and future lives.
	Demonstrate how their skills and talents contribute to their success.
	Discuss how their values and interests inform their decisions and actions.
Relationships	Engage in collaborative and mutually beneficial relationships to promote individual and group success.
	Assess when they need help from others and seek assistance.
	Demonstrate fairness, respect and equity in relationships with others.

EXAMPLE 6-D

Additional Sample CBA Competency Statements

Tables 6.1, 6.2 and 6.3 provide sample competency statements that are aligned with the CBA standards and informed by relevant contexts.

Table 6.1 Self-Direction Standard 2 (Elementary School)

Context	End-of-Level (6) Students will:	End-of-Grade (4) Students will:	End-of-Activity (3) Students will:
Student Planning	Describe effective and ineffective approaches to setting goals and planning, citing personal examples of each.	Describe one strength they have that helps them be successful in school.	Describe one goal they have set for Grade 3 and the steps they will take to reach it.
Academic Support	Articulate what they hope to learn in middle school that will be an important step to reaching their future successful self.	Describe two strategies they have used to overcome problems in school.	Articulate three choices they can make in school that will help them learn.
College and Career Readiness	Identify and describe two work values that are important to them.	Describe three skills that are important in a career that interests them.	Describe two careers that are related to their favorite school subjects.
Personal Growth	Summarize the personal traits that help them achieve success in school and the traits that could detract from their ability to be successful.	Describe a situation and the results in which they applied good judgment.	Describe how being prepared for school will help them be successful.
Social Interaction	Describe the skills that are necessary for a good partner or team member.	Describe the benefits of being a team player.	Explain the benefits of the following the "Give Respect/Get Respect" rule.

Table 6.2 Self-Direction Standard 2 (Middle School)

Context	End-of-Level (8) Students will:	End-of-Grade (7) Students will:	End-of-Activity (6) Students will:
Academic Support	Describe post-secondary aspirations and what they will need to do to meet them.	Describe how the educational choices they make now may affect their future plans.	Articulate personal learning style and list three strategies for adapting to other teaching styles.
College and Career Readiness	Evaluate their suitability/unsuitability for three different careers based upon knowledge of their own strengths, weaknesses, interests and attributes.	Articulate three personal strengths and interests and three possible careers that match them.	Describe their work values and three careers that match them.
Student Planning	Develop a plan for high school that incorporates knowledge of self, careers and high school career paths.	Describe personal attributes they have that will help them achieve their goals.	Articulate an academic, a career and a personal goal for the present school year and why they are important to their success.
Personal Growth	Describe how they will overcome adversity in high school with reference to examples of their greatest achievements in middle school.	Describe a personal challenge they encountered, how they overcame it and why it was important to their future success.	Describe two strategies for managing anger that they have used successfully.
Social Interaction	Identify an extra-curricular team/club they intend to join in high school and describe how it will contribute to their future success.	Describe the value of team work and their role in making a team successful.	Identify principles of nonviolence and how they apply to conflict resolution.

Table 6.3 Self-Direction Standard 2 (High School)

Self-Direction Standard 2 (High School) Competency Statements			
Students will demonstrate the self-direction, initiative, and skills necessary for achievement and success.			
Context	**End-of-Level (12) Students will:**	**End-of-Grade (10) Students will:**	**End-of-Activity (9) Students will:**
Academic Support	Describe how understanding their strengths has helped them in high school and how they will apply that knowledge to post-secondary success.	Describe their post-secondary interests and the personal attributes they have to help them succeed in them.	Describe a situation in which they made a difficult choice that led to a successful school achievement.
College and Career Readiness	Describe the personal factors that helped them succeed in high school and how they will help them in the career they plan to pursue.	Identify three possible careers that match their strengths and interests, and the educational requirements for each.	Describe their personality style and how knowing that can help them identify possible careers.
Student Planning	Describe how they will successfully use planning and goal setting in college based on the approaches they have successfully used in high school.	Describe how their choice of classes supports their possible future career.	Identify and describe two strengths they have that will help them reach their academic goals in Grade 9.
Personal Growth	Describe how they will overcome adversity in the future based on the identification of which strategies have worked and not worked for them in the past.	Describe a time in high school when their persistence worked to their advantage.	Describe a time when they felt depressed and the choices they made to overcome that feeling.
Social Interaction	Evaluate the skills they have in place and need to develop for being a contributing team member.	Describe how working in a study group contributed to their success in a team project.	Describe a situation in which they felt peer pressure and a strategy they utilized for a positive outcome.

7 Assessing Student Proficiency and Achievement in a CBA

Scenario 1

The school counselors in the Riverdell School District had been concerned that, while their program was accepted as an important part of the educational experience for all students, the accountability to which teachers were being held would at some point be applied to them as well. They met regularly and determined an approach that they believed would demonstrate the impact of their program. Each of the counselors collected data on various interventions and lessons that they implemented. At the end of the school year they presented the data to the administrators and faculty. It had been a time-consuming process and while well-received, they didn't think the amount of time involved was worth the nice, but underwhelming, response. They decided to collect some data the next year in case they needed it to demonstrate their work, but they had lost their enthusiasm about it.

Scenario 2

The school counselors in the Riverdell School District were implementing a Construct-Based Approach (CBA) to their school counseling program and were very enthusiastic about the results they expected for their students. They collected data to assess students' competency level, and to assess student gains after various interventions. Using the data generated from surveys and other assessments, they met to determine if they were being successful in the implementation of their program. At one such meeting, they wondered if the report card, which was being considered for revision, could be developed so that the behavior and skills section could reflect the constructs they were teaching in their program. They approached their supervisor, who in turn approached the superintendent, who thought the idea of a data-driven school counseling program had merit. The new report card was designed to include the constructs, and the school counselors were able to pull reports on their students each quarter and determine if the constructs were being learned and if they needed to hold small groups for some students who needed further instruction on the topics.

Reflections

The use of data is requisite for best practice in education. Having the constructs listed on a teacher-rated instrument (report card) gives school counselors the reports that they can use to make data-based decisions about their program for groups of students and individuals.

PURPOSE OF STUDENT EVALUATION

Student evaluation has been defined as the process of systematically collecting and interpreting information that can be used to inform students and their parents/guardians about the progress they are making toward attaining the knowledge, skills, attitudes and behaviors to be learned or acquired. Evaluation results inform the various personnel who make educational decisions (instructional, diagnostic, placement, promotion, graduation) about students (Joint Committee on Standards for Educational Evaluation, 2003).

There are at least three good reasons for the evaluation of student attainment of competencies and progress toward the standards.

First, it is necessary to be able to assess students' current levels of competency in order to make decisions about what types of interventions are needed to help them progress toward standards.

Second, it is necessary to be able to assess student gains after specific interventions in order to determine if these interventions are having their desired impact on students.

Third, it is necessary to be able to measure competency and standard attainment at graduation and at other points of transition (i.e., the terminal grades of elementary, middle school and/or junior high school) to determine if the school counseling program is achieving its goals and objectives, and to provide feedback to parents and students.

At each of these levels, there is also an obligation to provide relevant and useful assessment information to students, parents, and school colleagues and administrators. Students and parents deserve feedback on the competence levels of students. Parents deserve information on the gains associated with the school counseling activities in which children have been involved and the impact of the school counseling program, which they support with their taxes. Teachers deserve useful information about their students that will help them teach more effectively. Administrators deserve good information on the outcomes of school counseling interventions and the school counseling program to help them make informed decisions about resource allocation that will maximally benefit students.

CBA STUDENT PROFICIENCY ASSESSMENTS

A CBA requires assessment instruments, processes and systems that generate valid and useful information for the purposes of planning, decision making, communication and accountability. Figure 7.1 displays the student proficiency assessments discussed in this chapter.

The ability to accurately assess student progress, proficiency and achievement is critical to the design and successful implementation of a CBA. These four types of proficiency assessments, along with other sources

Figure 7.1 CBA Student Proficiency Assessments

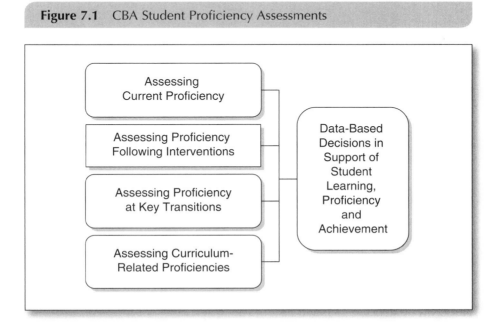

of student data (e.g., student information systems, data from intervention initiatives such as Response to Intervention) provide data that can be used in making data-informed decisions that support student learning, growth and development. Each assessment type is discussed below.

ASSESSING CURRENT LEVELS OF COMPETENCY

Assessments are needed to determine students' current levels of competency in relation to the CBA standards in order to make decisions about what types of interventions are needed to help them progress toward standards. This process may be thought of as a type of needs assessment where the framing of the student needs is based upon the essential competencies identified in the standards.

Traditionally, needs assessments have been based on common sense notions of what students need to know and be able to do. While helpful, such assessments do not provide maximally beneficial information since they are not aligned with competencies that are both teachable and known to be strongly related to academic achievement, school success and well-being. By aligning the needs assessment process with research-based standards, critical learning needs can be identified that are strongly related to the desired outcomes of public education. If these needs are met through the delivery of effective interventions concomitant gains in achievement, school success and student well-being are practically assured.

Needs assessment instruments should be developed to fit with students' age, experience, prior learning, prior mastery of competencies and material circumstances. The actual item must fit with the reading level of respondents.

Parent-Rated CBA Standards-Based Needs Assessment

A sample needs assessment for parents of late elementary school students to complete is provided in the Construction Zone at the end of this chapter. The assessment has 24 items that were written to correspond to research-based constructs that reflect student's Motivation (items 1–8), Self-Direction (items 15–20), Self-Knowledge (items 9–14) and Relationships (items 21–24). See the assessment instrument in the Construction Zone for a complete list of the 24 items in template form.

The items were written specifically for parents by intentionally selecting specific examples of behavior (My child can motivate him- or herself to do important things, for example, chores, homework, which are not necessarily fun) that parents are likely to be able to observe. In addition, the instructions invite parents to talk with their child before completing the assessment. Here, the intention is to help parents become better observers and become more knowledgeable about key success factors.

The items were written so as to reflect reasonable expectations of fifth- and sixth-grade students in a middle-class suburban community. A panel of fifth- and sixth-grade teachers was asked to screen and edit the items for developmental appropriateness. Finally, the items and directions were written in simple language (and reviewed and edited to increase simplicity) so that they would be readable and understandable by parents.

Following this simple process, standards-based needs assessments can be readily developed across the K–12 grade span and for a range of possible respondents (parents, teachers, students), each of whom has a unique perspective on the competencies of students. In most cases, gathering information from multiple types of respondents will result in a clearer picture of needs of students and the most important foci for school counseling interventions. The actual interventions can be designed by school counselors or selected from listings of research-based interventions (see Dimmitt, Carey, & Hatch, 2007, Chapter 4).

ASSESSING GAINS AFTER INTERVENTIONS

Whether specific interventions are selected or developed, it is necessary to be able to assess student gains after implementation in order to determine if these interventions have had their desired impact on students. This implementation evaluation requires that the competencies related to the construct that is the focus of the intervention be measured and compared (e.g., pre-intervention vs. post-intervention) to determine if change has occurred as a consequence of the intervention (see Dimmitt et al., 2007, Chapter 5).

Immediate, Proximal and Distal Student Outcomes

As Dimmitt et al. (2007) have noted, intervention evaluation and the selection of measures requires careful planning in order to assure the accuracy and utility of the results. It is important to note that all interventions can be expected to have several levels of outcomes, some of which are immediate, some proximal and some distal. For example, an intervention that is designed to help middle school students learn progressive relaxation techniques would be expected to result in better self-regulation of anxiety (immediate outcome), lower test anxiety on classroom tests (proximal outcome) and higher performance on achievement tests (distal outcome). While it would be tempting to just measure performance on the achievement tests to judge whether the intervention was successful, this would be problematic. Using distal outcome measures alone are not advised when the evaluation is based on a relatively small number of students (fewer than 250) for two related reasons.

First, most interventions are just not powerful enough for their effects to be readily evident in distal outcome measures. Second, distal outcomes are influenced by so many factors other than the intervention, that it is difficult to determine the impact of the intervention alone. Therefore it is advisable, in most school counseling intervention evaluation systems, to measure changes in immediate and proximal outcomes that reflect the actual construct-related competencies targeted by the intervention. Following a standards-based approach, these construct-related competencies will reflect aspects of motivation, self-direction, self-knowledge and relationships that are known to be related to positive outcomes for students (achievement, success and well-being).

It is helpful to plan the evaluation of an intervention by mapping out the relationships among the proximal and distal outcomes. The above example is represented in Figure 7.2.

It is generally advisable to choose to measure the targeted constructs that are closest to the intervention. In this example, the Self-Regulation of Emotions would be the desirable construct to measure. Because the standards are based on constructs that are connected to existing research traditions, it is relatively simple to find low- or no-cost measures that fit most constructs.

An online search of PsychINFO using the keywords "self-regulation," "emotion," "scale" and "children" surfaced an article on the psychometric properties of the Children's Emotion Management Scales (Zeman, Shipman, & Penza-Clyve, 2001) and an article on the development of the Children's Emotional Management Checklist (Shields & Cicchetti, 1997). The Children's Emotional Management Scales is a child self-report measure that consists of subscales reflecting children's abilities to manage sadness and anger.

Figure 7.2   Measuring Changes in Immediate and Proximal Outcomes

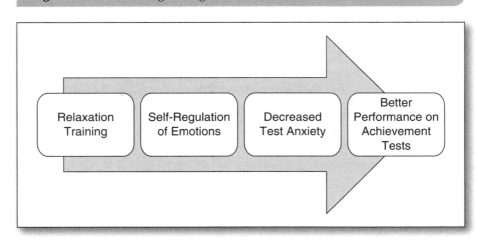

The Children's Emotional Management Checklist is a parent-rating form that measures both children's level of inappropriate expression of emotion and the child's ability to regulate emotions effectively (characterized by appropriate emotional expression, empathy and emotional self-awareness). Both scales have been used effectively with children as young as 8 years old.

Both of these scales would be useful measures of the effectiveness of an elementary school counseling intervention that was designed to increase students' abilities to effectively manage negative emotions.

There are several additional useful sources for identifying scales that would be valuable for measuring changes in students' construct-related abilities after school counseling interventions. These include:

Google Scholar (http://scholar.google.com)

The Collaborative for Academic Social and Emotional Learning website (http://casel.org) and publications (e.g., Denham, Ji, & Hamre, 2010).

Buros Institute of Mental Measurements test reviews online (http://buros .unl.edu/buros/jsp/search.jsp)

In general, finding existing scales that measure constructs related to motivation, self-determination and relationships will be relatively easy. A list of several additional useful scales related to each of these three domains is provided in the Construction Zone at the end of this chapter.

Measuring self-knowledge-related constructs, however, will generally require that school counselors develop their own pre-/post- surveys to measure students' self-knowledge. The accuracy and extent of a person's self-knowledge can really only be judged by how accurately it reflects and explicates genuine aspects of the self. It is virtually impossible to develop a standardized instrument that measures each respondent's knowledge of himself or herself.

The closest approximation to such an instrument can be found in the family of self-efficacy instruments that measure the extent to which individuals are confident that they have the ability to do something that is based in part on some adequate level of self-knowledge in a given domain. If students report that they are confident that they can make good career decisions, for example, it is reasonable to assume that they are basing their self-efficacy belief, at least, in part, on a self-assessment that they have adequate knowledge of themselves in order to make good career decisions.

Alternatively, if students' levels of self-efficacy for career decision making change after a self-knowledge focused intervention, it is reasonable to assume that this change results from gains in self-knowledge. So, standardized self-efficacy measures can be used as a proxy for actual measures of self-knowledge.

In general, however, it will be better to construct measures of self-knowledge that can be administered before and after an intervention to assess the gains that are related to the intervention. An effective process of developing such measures is thoroughly described in Dimmitt et al. (2007; see Chapter 7). Basically, this process would involve first identifying the key self-knowledge constructs that are the target of the intervention. This involves a precise statement of what concepts were intended to be learned and at which level of mastery (e.g., knowledge, comprehension, application and evaluation) it was intended that they be learned. This information is typically derived from the competency statements (learning objectives) of the intervention.

Next, it is important to select an item format (e.g., multiple choice, fill in the blank) that will allow students to express their learning through their responses. Then, it is necessary to develop multiple knowledge-based items related to each construct. Each item must be edited for clarity and readability based on feedback from colleagues. It is helpful to have a colleague and some "test" students read through and give feedback on the items in order to catch possible problems with reading level and/or potential misinterpretation of the items. Finally, it is important to write similar, clear instructions for the survey.

If the same survey is administered before and after the intervention, gains in self-knowledge can be determined.

Constructs related to self-knowledge reflect a number of areas where research indicates such knowledge may be related to increased academic achievement, success and enhanced well-being. These areas include knowledge of one's own current abilities and strengths in different domains for both academic and nonacademic endeavors. A realistic assessment of current strengths and weaknesses is critically important in career and educational planning. It is a critical foundation for personal decision making.

It is also important for students to develop self-knowledge in terms of how they approach learning new material. Here, knowledge of both their general cognitive styles and their specific learning styles is important. Such knowledge helps students choose learning environments that are best suited to their preferred approach to learning and construct personalized study approaches and strategies that are most likely to be effective.

It is also very helpful if students know which activities they find to be intrinsically interesting to them and which activities (that they may need to perform) are not intrinsically interesting. Knowledge of intrinsic interests is important in career and educating planning. Being able to identify necessary activities that are not intrinsically interesting is an important foundation for learning how to motivate one's self to do things that one does not find intrinsically interesting.

Relatedly, it is also important to help students identify how they typically make sense of their successes and failures so that they can develop a more realistic appraisal of them and acquire more effective approaches to building on their success and learning from their failures. This type of "causal attribution" learning is particularly important for students who have fallen into the pattern of protecting themselves from experiencing failure (e.g., bad grades on a test) by attributing the cause of their failure to things that are outside their control (e.g., a mean teacher) rather than to things that are within their control (e.g., not studying enough). Being able to name and recognize a self-defeating pattern of behavior is an essential step in changing it.

Knowledge of one's preferred decision-making style is also a very valuable aspect of self-knowledge. Likewise, knowledge of personal values is very important since values serve as the standards upon which major life decisions are based. Focusing on the self-knowledge foundations of decision making is critically important in order to equip students to learn how to make important life decisions.

Finally, it is very helpful for students to know their own stable personality and temperament characteristics. It is also very helpful if they understand the personality and temperament of others. For example, it is extremely useful for high school students to understand that some people are naturally extroverts and some naturally introverts. This foundational knowledge is essential to their development of self-acceptance, understanding of others, and the development of personal strategies to negotiate the social world of adolescence that are consistent with personal tendencies and strengths.

To avoid confusion, it should be noted that a number of scales do exist that measure these types of constructs (e.g., the numerous self-rating scales that measure career interests). The purpose of these scales, however, is to facilitate the development of self-knowledge rather than to measure the acquisition of self-knowledge. A career interest scale, for example, is often used as part of an intervention to promote self-knowledge. Such a scale, however, would be virtually useless as a pre-/post- measure of actual knowledge gained as a consequence of the intervention. A separate instrument developed specifically for this proposes would be necessary.

ASSESSING PROGRESS TOWARD STANDARDS AT KEY TRANSITION POINTS

As noted above, it is important to be able to measure competency and standard attainment at graduation and at other points of transition (i.e., the terminal grades of elementary, middle school and/or junior high school) to determine if the CBA school counseling program is achieving its goals and objectives. It is also important to make such assessments periodically in order to provide feedback to parents and students on how students are progressing toward standards.

Most schools already use report cards to accomplish these purposes. Traditional report cards typically include indicators of academic competence (e.g., grades in history, math and art) and behavior that is considered to be related to academic achievement (e.g., works well with other students, completes assigned homework). This practice reflects the common sense notion that useful report cards should reflect not only academic performance, but also students' behavior that is related to their abilities to learn effectively.

In recent years, the development of standards-based report cards has become more common. These report cards reference student academic learning directly to specified state and/or district standards. These report cards also typically include teachers' ratings of students on behavior that is generally considered to be related to academic achievement. Since 2005, for example, the entire state of Hawaii has been using a standards-based report card (Hawaii Department of Education, 2013). In addition to evaluating performance on academic subjects, this card evaluates areas such as becoming a self-directed learner, showing good problem solving and being an effective communicator.

There are two problems with behavioral components of traditional report cards. First, the behaviors that are reported are not selected systematically and do not necessarily reflect research on personal, emotional and social factors that are intimately related to achievement and success. Second, teachers are asked to make ratings of student behavior without reference to a rubric that would ensure the reliability of these ratings. In short, the information on student characteristics may be neither valid nor reliable.

Standards-based report cards reflect the same "validity" problem related from a failure to align the identified student characteristics with research on constructs related to achievement. Typically, however, the "reliability" of teacher ratings on standards-based report cards is enhanced by rubrics that specify age-appropriate criteria for categorizing student behavior.

We recommend the use of a construct-based behavioral section of report cards that will provide grade-level information on student attainment of competencies. We recommend that these ratings be made with reference to grade-level rubrics that define the meaning of the construct at that grade level and provide concrete examples of student behavior characteristic of each level of the rating scale (e.g., "Needs Improvement," "On Target," "Strength").

Such a construct-related approach will result in the development of behavioral sections of report cards that reflect the most important student behaviors related to achievement and that provide accurate reliable information on the current levels of performance of students. Construct-based student behavior sections can be incorporated into either traditional or standards-based report cards and will add to the value of both.

There are several good reasons to incorporate an assessment of the constructs that form the basis of school counseling standards into students' report cards. Doing so:

Enables the identification of students who are progressing well in terms of the development of necessary abilities related to achievement and success and the identification of students who are struggling to develop such abilities. The identification of struggling students enables the application of school counseling interventions where they are most needed.

Provides valuable information to students and parents about the development of critical success-oriented abilities.

Enables the evaluation of school counseling program activities by making valuable data accessible by incorporating its collection into the everyday routines of the school. Such data can be used to assess the short-term outcomes of specific interventions (by assessing how many students move from "Needs Improvement" to "On Target") or the longer-term evaluation of the school counseling program (by documenting the construct-related learning of students over time).

Sensitizes teachers, parents and students to notice important aspects of student behavior that are related to achievement and success. Counselors can then work more effectively with teachers, parents and students to help them develop ways to promote students' development in critical areas.

Increases the visibility of the student outcomes of the school counseling program for all major stakeholders.

Developing Construct-Based Report Cards

Given the diversity among schools and districts, it is not advisable that all schools adopt a common construct-based report card. It is important that districts develop their own report cards based upon local conditions and expectations. Because behavioral report card items require a high level of inference on the part of teachers, an accompanying scoring rubric with behavioral descriptors of exemplary behavior for each performance level is also necessary.

Behavioral report cards are best developed by a team of experienced teachers (who will have precise knowledge of readily observable behavior at different grade levels) led by the school counselor (who will have precise knowledge of constructs that are known to be related to achievement, success and well-being). It is helpful to start following these steps:

- Select the rating scale.

- Select and define the most salient constructs.

- Develop the scoring rubric.

- Get feedback from parents in terms of information quality and utility.

- Get feedback from teachers in terms of feasibility and utility.

- Revise the report card and rubric.

- Pilot implementing the new report card for a year.

- Evaluate by seeking teacher, parent and student feedback.

- Selecting the Rating Scale

In general, three- or four-level rating scales represent the best balance between information quality and reliability. A good three-level rating scale would use "Needs Improvement," "On Target" and "Strength." "On Target" reflects expected performance. "Needs Improvement" indicates that this is a problematic area for the student and requires some attention. "Strength" reflects a special ability of the student that exceeds expectations for age-level behavior. While it is tempting to develop more complex and differentiated rating systems, such systems strain human capacity to make accurate judgments, require additional time and tend to be less reliable.

Selecting and Defining the Most Salient Constructs

Based on knowledge of the constructs and standards, the team next selects and defines the most salient items that are related to the grade level and particular climate and context of the district or school. For 12th grade, these construct definitions should reflect the terminal-level competencies that all students are expected to have when graduating from the district. For other grades, these construct definitions reflect approximations to these terminal competencies (grade and level competencies). This process is infinitely easier if grade, level, and terminal competency statements have been developed in advance.

Developing the Scoring Rubric

Once the items have been developed, the team can create a draft of the scoring rubric. The purpose of the rubric is to allow teachers to accurately and reliable differentiate between different levels of performance on each item. Accuracy and reliability are best achieved through behavioral anchoring—the use of observable behavior descriptions of behavior characteristic of each level of performance. In general, it is best to first draft the rubric for the expected level of performance ("On Target") then move on to rubric areas that describe behavior reflective of exceeding ("Strength") and failing to reach ("Needs Improvement") the desired level of performance. A sample scoring rubric for the first item is presented in Table 7.1.

Once the team develops the report card and rubric, a series of field tests and related revisions are conducted, including a review by parent and teachers of the

Table 7.1 Sample Rubric for Motivation: Actively Participate in Class Activities.

Needs Improvement	On Target	Strength
→ The student is frequently not engaged in learning activities in the classroom. → The student frequently appears disinterested, attends to other things during the learning activity, loses track of the activity, and cannot recall what happened or what was learned. → The student's participation level is impeding the development of understanding learning.	→ The student is most often engaged appropriately in the learning activities in the classroom. → Evidence for active engagement includes demonstrating attention, staying on track, asking relevant questions, volunteering information, being able to recall the activity and being able to identify what was learned. → The student's participation level supports understanding and learning.	→ The student is nearly always engaged appropriately in learning activities in the classroom. → Instances of lack of engagement are almost non-existent. The student often anticipates what will happen next in the activity and appears highly motivated to learn. → The student's participation level is promoting a deep level of understanding and learning.

draft documents and a pilot implementation and evaluation. Once fully implemented, the construct-based report card will result in better information for parents and students on student progress toward standards for important achievement-related aspects of behavior. This is an efficient way for counselors to identify students who need particular types of supports for effective learning—and an efficient way to evaluate the student outcomes of the counseling program.

ASSESSING CURRICULUM-RELATED PROFICIENCIES

Student assessments embedded in CBA school counseling curriculum activities can be used to assess student progress, proficiency and achievement. The primary benefit of curriculum-related proficiencies is that the student assessments provide immediate feedback for students regarding their performance in relation to specific competencies. Providing such feedback is a critical educational strategy as it a) identifies specific areas in need of improvement for individual students; b) provides an opportunity to discuss the learning deficits with the student while the learning experience is still fresh in the student's mind; c) encourages students to look at their own learning, thinking and behavior processes and how to improve them; and d) engages students in defining and implementing action steps (with due dates) to improve both their learning processes and the amount of specific content required in the curriculum activity.

Competencies are proficiency-building results that serve as the foundation of CBA curriculum activities. They are specific learning targets students are expected to achieve. Students work toward becoming proficient by acquiring knowledge relevant to the content of the competency statement (specific knowledge and skills) and developing skills needed to successfully apply the knowledge in a variety of authentic contexts. The core CBA curriculum is an integrated set of proficiency-building activities that collectively provide the learning opportunities through which students participating in the program can achieve the CBA school counseling student standards.

The importance of immediate feedback to students based on assessment results in CBA curriculum activities cannot be overstated. This is the juncture at which students can most benefit from reflecting on their learning processes and determine what they can do to improve their learning outcomes. It is a time when students with poor or failing grades will be most focused on the harsh consequences of doing poorly or failing in school. School counselors in a CBA program utilize the feedback loop to identify, communicate and act to resolve the learning deficits evident in the student assessment results.

Every documented CBA curriculum activity has embedded assessments. This is to demonstrate that student learning in relation to the specified competencies can be assessed and by what means. Three types of data are considered in CBA activities: process data (what is done for whom?), perception data (what do people perceive about the process and its impact?) and results data (what is the quality of the work and its impact?). The results from these three types of data are triangulated to more accurately determine students' individual learning strengths and deficits.

Every CBA core curriculum activity has embedded assessments that provide tangible ways to assess student progress toward the stated competencies for the activity. This provides counselors with immediate insights into how well students are performing (demonstrating what they know and can do as a result of participating in the activity), and enables them to provide immediate feedback to students regarding their strengths and areas in need of improvement.

In addition to individual assessments used with counseling activities, counselors also review the quality of student portfolio entries and individual learning plans as evidence of progress toward the CBA student standards. The final test of the impact of delivering the curriculum, however, is that students graduate from high school with good grades, a clear sense of what they want to do following graduation, and the knowledge and skills they need to succeed in the post-secondary world.

How Student Proficiency is Determined

In short, student proficiency is determined by using data that demonstrates a student has a) participated in the curriculum activities, b) met the expected results for the curriculum activity and c) produced artifacts based on rigorous acceptance criteria. Accurate student outcome data is required in order to demonstrate the impact of the CBA program.

When Have Students Achieved the CBA Standards?

The following statements summarize what a student should know and be able to do as a result of participating in a CBA counseling program:

– Acquire knowledge, skills and attitudes that lead to lifelong success.

– Prepare for, and make informed decisions about, post-secondary opportunities.

– Understand the importance of school to a successful future.

– Develop a positive self-image and recognition of their ability.

– Plan for their future by understanding the requirements for success, setting meaningful goals and taking necessary steps to achieve them.

Four sources of data are used to determine whether students are achieving the CBA standards:

Level of Student Participation in Curriculum

A student's ability to demonstrate proficiency depends on participating in the learning opportunities provided through the CBA curriculum. The focus of data gathering is on whether students have acquired the knowledge, developed the skills and embraced appropriate attitudes and behaviors as a result of participating in the counseling curriculum. Students cannot be expected to demonstrate their learning if they have not been available to learn what to do and how to do it.

Curriculum-Related Assessment Results

Data from curriculum-based student assessments are an important source of information about an individual student's learning needs and the impact of delivering interventions to help students improve their learning processes.

Artifacts and Other Products Completed to Meet Learning Targets

The production and presentation of artifacts, or other items produced by the student, are the primary means students have to demonstrate what they know and can do as a result of their learning. The district defines a rigorous set of criteria that have to be met in order for an artifact to be accepted as part of a graduation requirement. It is assumed that any artifact that has been accepted has already met rigorous standards and therefore can be considered evidence of a student's proficiency.

School counselors have a predefined list of graduation artifacts that are required of all students (e.g., written year-end reflection, career exploration project).

Student Scores on CBA Proficiency Assessments

Student scores on the other proficiency assessments discussed in this chapter are also a good source of data on student proficiency and achievement.

A student can be said to have achieved the CBA standards from participating in the school counseling program by demonstrating proficiency in each of these areas. Making this determination requires providing students with multiple opportunities for rigorous learning and applying their learning to authentic contexts, and meaningful opportunities to demonstrate what they know and can do as a result of the CBA program.

IMPORTANCE OF LINKING CBA TO RESEARCH-BASED CONSTRUCTS

The major assessment functions associated with a data-driven CBA school counseling program can be made much more effective by linking them to standards that are rooted in research-based constructs. Such linkages ensure that research on factors affecting achievement, success and well-being drives the needs assessment process and helps determine the foci of the school counseling program. Such linkages ensure that interventions are selected and evaluated in terms of their ability to promote achievement, success and well-being.

Finally, such linkages ensure that the school counseling program is evaluated in terms of its ability to promote known motivational, self-direction, self-knowledge and relationship factors that underlay students' success in school and in life. In addition, using a consistent language based on defined constructs in all these assessment will promote communication and understanding among counselors, teachers, parents and students about important student abilities that are necessary for their success and within the domain of responsibility of the school counseling program.

Chapter 7
CONSTRUCTION ZONE
Thinking Hard Hats Required

CONNECTING CHAPTER 7 TO TOOLKIT CONSTRUCTION SITE 3

School counseling programs are designed to support students' pursuit of excellence through the delivery of meaningful learning opportunities and responsive services that address developmental, personal and social needs. Student assessments are a primary building block for a CBA. These assessments are critical because they help determine student progress toward, and achievement of, the standards and competencies established for them. Student data is valuable information that is needed to guide student learning and help students assume ownership for their own learning. Construction Site 3 helps you look at some key aspects of student assessments in a CBA.

As a result of completing Construction Site 3 tasks, you can expect to learn and do the following:

- ✓ Learn what it means for a student to demonstrate proficiency and achievement in a CBA school counseling program, and ways in which they can be assessed.

- ✓ Learn about the need for a school counseling data management system.

- ✓ Review examples of student assessments that can be used in a CBA.

- ✓ Learn about a CBA as a standards-based program.

- ✓ Review a proposed section on student report cards based on CBA school counseling student standards.

- ✓ Learn how student assessments are linked to CBA standards and competencies.

- ✓ Learn about the role of data and data-based decision making in a CBA.

- ✓ Develop a plan for establishing and integrating a CBA to student assessment into your current program.

- ✓ Use sample CBA assessment instruments as models for developing similar types of instruments for your program.

Looking forward to seeing you at
Toolkit Construction Site 3!

EXAMPLE 7-A

Parent-Rated Standards-Based Student Needs Assessment

Sample Form Letter to Parents

Dear Parent,

Listed below are 24 statements about characteristics of elementary school students that are known to be associated with academic achievement and the development of a sense of well-being. Please indicate the degree to which you agree or disagree with each statement with respect to your own child's current capabilities. For some of these statements, it may be helpful to talk with your child before responding. This information will be used to plan school counseling activities to develop these characteristics, and thereby, support your child's growth and development.

Thank you.

Needs Assessment Instrument

#	Item	Strongly Disagree	Disagree	Agree	Strongly Agree
1	My child can identify his/her most favorite and least favorite subjects at school.				
2	My child can identify his/her most favorite and least favorite recreational activities.				
3	My child can name at least one possible future occupation that fits with his/her favorite subjects or activities.				
4	My child can describe at least one occupation that s/he could see her-/himself following.				
5	My child can describe his/her ideal home life situation when s/he is an adult.				

#	Item	Strongly Disagree	Disagree	Agree	Strongly Agree
6	My child can describe a possible situation in the future that s/he fears and would work to avoid.				
7	My child can motivate him-/herself to do necessary things (e.g., chores, homework) that are not fun.				
8	My child can do his/her household chores with minimal reminders.				
9	My child can describe ways that his/her personality is different from his/her friends.				
10	My child can describe things that s/he can do better than most of his/her friends.				
11	My child can describe things most of his/her friends can do better than him/her.				
12	My child can describe things that s/he is interested in that his/her friends are not.				
13	My child can identify at least one human characteristic (e.g., courage, charity, kindness) that s/he values.				
14	My child can identify at least one type of activity (e.g., sports, learning, relating with others) that s/he enjoys.				
15	My child can describe at least one incident when s/he was successful at something because of his/her innate gift or talent.				

(Continued)

(Continued)

#	Item	Strongly Disagree	Disagree	Agree	Strongly Agree
16	My child can describe at least one incident when s/he was successful at something because of perseverance and effort.				
17	My child can describe at least one incident where s/he was unsuccessful at something because s/he failed to work hard enough at it.				
18	My child can describe at least one strategy s/he uses to learn or remember something.				
19	My child is able to describe at least one strategy s/he uses to calm him-/herself when s/he is anxious or upset.				
20	My child is able to rebound from disappointments, setbacks and failures, and continue to work toward a goal.				
21	My child is able to collaborate well with other children to achieve mutual goals.				
22	My child can identify at least two different people that s/he would ask for help corresponding to two different types of needs for help (e.g., help with math homework vs. help with a friendship issue).				
23	My child spontaneously talks about situations in school where s/he believes someone was treated unfairly.				
24	My child spontaneously talks about situations in society where s/he believes someone was treated unfairly.				

EXAMPLE 7-B

Additional Assessment Scales

(http://buros.unl.edu/buros/jsp/search.jsp)

In general, finding existing scales that measure constructs related to motivation, self-determination and relationships will be relatively easy. A list of several additional useful scales related to each of these three domains is presented in Table 7.2 below:

Table 7.2 Examples of Assessment Scales that Measure CBA Constructs

Standards Domain	Scales and Instrument	Age Range	Reference
Motivation	Intrinsic Goal Orientation and Extrinsic Goal Orientation subscales of the Motivated Strategies for Learning Questionnaire	Student self-report, 7th grade and older	Pintrich & DeGroot (1990)
	Motivation, Intrinsic Motivation and Extrinsic Motivation subscales of the Academic Motivation Scale	Student self-report, high school	Vallerand et al. (1992) Cokley, Bernard, Cunningham, & Motoike (2001)
Self-Direction	Self-Direction of Learning and Self-Regulation of Arousal subscales of the Student Engagement in School Success Skills Survey	Student self-report, 5th grade and older	Carey, Brigman, Webb, Villares, & Harrington (in press)
	Metacognitive Self-Regulation subscale of the Motivated Strategies for Learning Questionnaire	Student self-report, 7th grade and older	Pintrich & DeGroot (1990)
	Emotion Regulation subscale of the Emotion Regulation Checklist	Teacher or Parent rating, preschool and older	Shields et al. (2001)

(Continued)

Table 7.2 (Continued)

Standards Domain	Scales and Instrument	Age Range	Reference
Relationships	Support of Classmates Learning subscale of the Student Engagement in School Success Skills Survey	Student self-report, 5th grade and older	Carey et al. (in press)
	Help-Seeking subscale of the Motivated Strategies for Learning Questionnaire	Student self-report, 7th grade and older.	Pintrich & DeGroot (1990)
	Social Competence subscale of the School Social Behavior Scales	Teacher rating, K–12	Merrell (1993)

EXAMPLE 7-C

Example of a Grade 2 Construct-Based Report Card

Construct	Student Behavior Related to Academic Achievement	Needs Improvement	On Target	Strength
Motivation	Actively participates in class activities			
	Demonstrate perseverance on difficult tasks			
	Can describe a positive vision of the future			
	Able to identify activities he/she enjoys when given choices			
Self-Knowledge	Identifies their own personal feelings			
	Identifies their own academic strengths			
	Identifies things they are interested in learning			
	Identifies human qualities (e.g. courage, kindness) that they value			
Self –Direction	Is actively engaged in classroom work			
	Organizes workspace and materials			
	Uses learning strategies			
	Demonstrates ability to self-regulate negative emotions			
Relationships	Cooperates with others			
	Shows Respect for others			
	Forms good relationships with peers			
	Asks for help when needed			

8 CBA Program Implementation

Focus on Planning

Scenario 1

Keisha and Maria attended a national school counseling conference where they learned so many exciting new ideas about developing a school counseling program in which they would teach their students new knowledge and skills to help them succeed. They shared their new knowledge each evening and vowed to work together when they returned to their school to embrace their new learning and develop and implement a program that would make an important difference for their students. Upon returning to school, they approached their principal with their ideas and excitedly explained how they planned to implement a new program. Their principal was happy to hear their enthusiasm and wished them well. However, he also noted that they had a lot on their plate already with the state testing season about to commence and, of course, they must be sure every student had an appropriate schedule and all student records were up to date. And, by the way, what were they doing about contacting parents of truant students? Keisha and Maria were determined to move forward and began to develop the outline of a program as best they could between all of the duties they were assigned. The school year ended before they were able to complete the program design, and they hoped they would have time to work on it in the summer and early fall.

Scenario 2

Keisha and Maria had learned about the Construct-Based Approach (CBA) to school counseling programs in their graduate program. At the end of their first year as school counselors, they went to a school counseling conference and attended several sessions that ignited their enthusiasm about redesigning their school's program to include this approach. They returned to school and outlined the research that backed the construct-based approach and a detailed plan for developing and implementing for their principal. The principal was intrigued by the claims the research made on student achievement and impressed by the plan his counselors had developed. He allowed the counselors time to develop their program by reducing their non-counseling duties. By the second quarter of the school year, Keisha and Maria were ready to begin implementation of a pilot in the ninth grade. At year's end, they gave a presentation to their administrators and faculty on the results achieved. Teachers supported the results with anecdotes of their own based on their observations of student progress in some of the identified areas. The program was accepted as an excellent addition to the school and expanded to include all students in all grades. Within a few years, Keisha and Maria had no non-counseling duties and were training other school counselors in their district on developing a construct-based program.

Reflections

Both the research base and the road map the CBA to school counseling have to offer make the process of developing a program and having it accepted by administration easier. Having a well-developed plan ensures that the work will get done.

SHIFT IN FOCUS FROM BUILDING TO IMPLEMENTING A CBA

Chapters 1 and 2 introduced the construct-based approach (CBA) to school counseling and provided a simple language set by which to describe and discuss a CBA to school counseling. Chapters 3–7 described five building blocks of a CBA: research-based constructs, relevant contexts, student results (standards and competencies), curriculum delivery and student assessments.

Now that we have seen how a CBA is built, it is time to shift our focus to implementing a CBA. Chapters 8–11 focus on taking the CBA program defined in the first seven chapters and implementing it. Chapter 8 focuses on developing plans to implement a CBA. Chapter 9 focuses on delivering the CBA with fidelity and data management. Chapter 10 focuses on evaluating the efficacy and impact of the CBA. Chapter 11 shows how the CBA can interact with other national school improvement initiatives. Collectively, these chapters illustrate the importance and outcomes of a well-designed CBA implementation process.

A CBA is results based. As noted in "A Vision to Live By" in Chapter 5, primary results expected from implementing a CBA are that students will become highly motivated, self-directed learners who are knowledgeable about themselves and are engaged as contributors to the well-being of our world. Helping students achieve these results requires an effective planning process to define expected results, develop action plans, implement the plans and monitor progress, and evaluate the impact of implementing the CBA program.

HOW TO BEGIN

Figure 8.1 shows the five building blocks of a CBA. While engaged in the process of using the building blocks to develop the content of a construct-based approach in your own school, it is also important to think about what is required to successfully deliver the program and evaluate its impact.

The figure also indicates four critical implementation processes discussed in Chapters 8 through 11. Completion of these processes enables

Figure 8.1 How to Begin Implementing a CBA

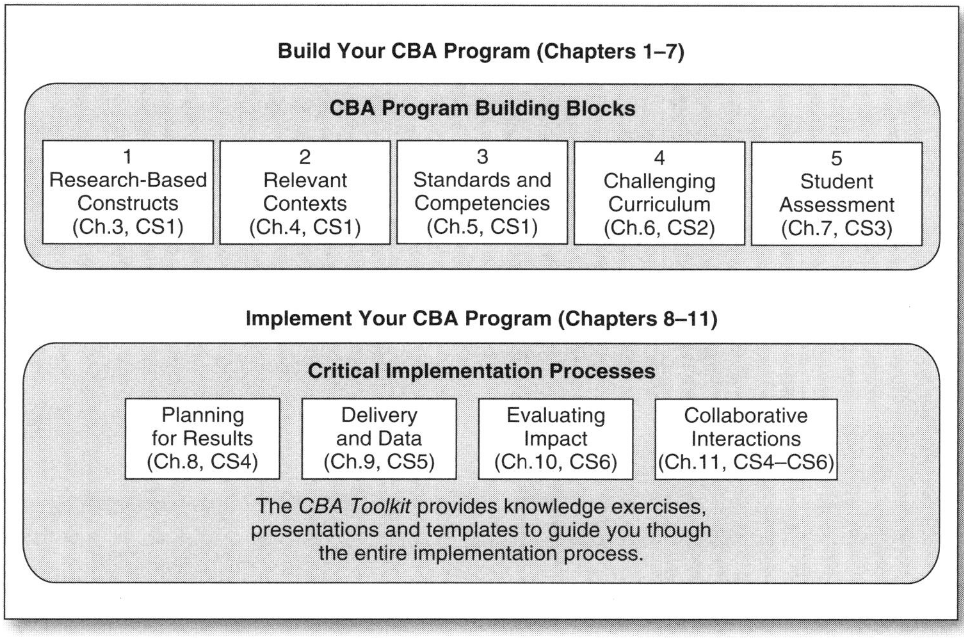

Build Your CBA Program (Chapters 1–7)

CBA Program Building Blocks

1 Research-Based Constructs (Ch.3, CS1)	2 Relevant Contexts (Ch.4, CS1)	3 Standards and Competencies (Ch.5, CS1)	4 Challenging Curriculum (Ch.6, CS2)	5 Student Assessment (Ch.7, CS3)

Implement Your CBA Program (Chapters 8–11)

Critical Implementation Processes

Planning for Results (Ch.8, CS4)	Delivery and Data (Ch.9, CS5)	Evaluating Impact (Ch.10, CS6)	Collaborative Interactions (Ch.11, CS4–CS6)

The *CBA Toolkit* provides knowledge exercises, presentations and templates to guide you though the entire implementation process.

school counselors to develop results-based plans, implement them, monitor progress, make adjustments as needed and evaluate the extent to which the expected results have been achieved. The alignment of the five building blocks and four implementation processes with book chapters and *CBA Toolkit* Construction Sites are provided in the figure.

See the Construction Zone at the end of this chapter for a list of tools in the *CBA Toolkit* that can be used in conjunction with this chapter.

WHY ALL THE FUSS ABOUT PLANNING?

Planning is a critical skill that involves envisioning the future, goal setting, decision making, problem solving, self-regulation and self-reflection. The need to plan (how to get from Point A to Point B) is ever-present in our lives and learning. It is impossible to get from Point A to Point B in life without some type of planning. Even the act of defining Point A (where we are now) and Point B (where we want to be) is an essential function in the planning process. Planning is a transferable skill that can be applied in productive ways in every aspect of student learning.

Planning processes are critical to metacognitive and executive function skill development which, in turn, are critical to school counselors' ability to support students' academic achievement. Teaching students to envision their possible selves and plan for their future success is a focus for school counselors in a CBA school counseling program.

THREE PERSPECTIVES ON THE PLANNING PROCESS

Chapter 8 focuses on the first CBA implementation process listed in Figure 8.1: Planning for Results. There is no substitute for effective front-end planning, and it is important for school counselors to become proficient planners as a core professional responsibility. This section discusses three perspectives on the planning processes that are relevant to school counselors planning a CBA for their school's counseling program: a) Four Basic Questions, b) A Complete Planning Cycle and c) Continuous Improvement.

Four Basic Questions

Planning is about identifying future results to be achieved, figuring out the best way to achieve them, taking the initiative to act, and demonstrating the ability to self-reflect on, and learn from, one's experiences. Planning is conducted by answering four basic questions:

- **Where do we want to be?** A CBA is results based. The first step in planning for a CBA is to clearly define the results that can be expected from implementing the program. School counselors need to engage in dialog about their vision of student excellence and how to help students achieve what is expected of them.

- **Where are we now?** Once standards of excellence have been established, the next question looks at the current counseling program in relation to the standards (where we want to be). It is important for school counselors to conduct both needs and capability assessments to determine the gap between the current and ideal programs, and to determine the school's capacity for implementing a CBA.

- **How do we get from here to there?** Once the gap has been defined, the next question involves how to get from the current to the ideal program. This is where plan development is a key process in the successful implementation of a CBA. School counselors need to be proficient at planning for the school counseling program and their personal role in fulfilling the mission of the program.

- **How do we measure our results?** This is one of the most important questions that can be asked about a CBA program as the intent of a CBA is to make a difference in the lives of the students and families served by school counselors. It is impossible to know the impact of a CBA without effective measures. Without data on the impact of the program, it is difficult to maximize counselors' potential for building student proficiency and supporting their academic achievement. The answers to this question are especially critical to the continuous improvement perspective discussed later in this section.

These four questions are used to generate information needed to successfully complete the planning cycle for CBA school counseling programs.

A Complete Planning Cycle

Planning for a CBA is so much more than simply writing down some goals and action steps and calling it a day. It is important to remember that planning is a complete cycle of activities for defining results, developing and implementing action plans, and monitoring and evaluating the impact of implementing the CBA and using the evaluation results to update and/or create new plans.

A simple way to look at planning is that the plan evolves from looking for anything in the school counseling program that is in need of improvement, articulating them as needs statements and transforming them into results statements to be achieved. The results statements form the basis of all action plans. The plans represent what the school/district will attempt to accomplish to diminish and/or eliminate the gap between the current and ideal programs.

Figure 8.2 shows the phases and activities in a complete planning cycle for school counseling programs.

Figure 8.2 A Complete Planning Cycle

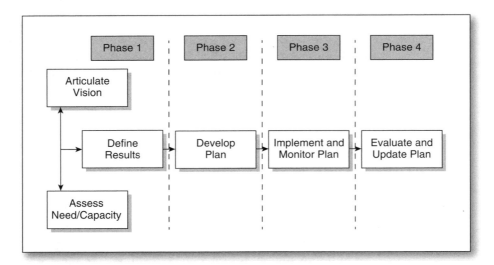

All four phases are critical to the success of the planning effort. Phase 1 begins with defining the results that can be expected from implementing a CBA program. These standards for program excellence form the basis of needs/capability assessments that determine the gap between the current and the ideal programs. The output of a needs assessment is articulated as need statements that are easily rewritten as results statements. The focus of a needs statement on specifying current need shifts to a focus on a future result that when achieved will address the need.

For example, a needs statement might be "Career development lessons are inconsistently delivered in every grade." This can translate to a results statement: "A K–12 career development strand is fully implemented in all grades."

Phase 2 develops the plan. The expected results for the various parts of the plan have been identified in Phase 1, and it is now time to develop action steps to achieve the results and measure the impact of the plan being implemented. Clearly defined results, action steps and effective measures are essential functions when planning for a CBA.

Effective planning requires attention to areas critical to the success of a CBA program. For example, targeted areas might include instruction and assessment, CBA curriculum development, organizational support, school counseling data management, family and community engagement, and professional development.

Each of these areas requires a set of planning, delivery and evaluation processes capable of establishing sustainable CBA processes. A CBA program can be implemented in a variety of ways, from incremental to full implementation. It is important to remember that a CBA reflects changes in the way school counselors view their students by focusing on motivation, self-direction, self-knowledge and relationships. Developed plans should reflect these core aspects of implementing a CBA.

In Phase 3, the plan is implemented and progress monitored, making adjustments as needed throughout the process. The plan identifies primary responsibilities for the successful completion of the plan and its implementation, and a timeframe within which the results are to be achieved. Ongoing progress monitoring is essential to delivering the highest-quality CBA program. Formative assessments are used throughout Phase 3.

Phase 4 is an annual summative assessment that takes a close look at the accomplishments and challenges of the current school year and generates information that can be used to update plans and/or create new plans. The results of the evaluation should be documented, presented and distributed to those who need the information to make informed decisions about the CBA school counseling program.

Continuous Improvement

Continuous improvement principles are incorporated into the plan to ensure ongoing monitoring of progress toward the plan's expected results and timely adjustments to implementation activities to resolve immediate needs.

Figure 8.3 displays the continuous improvement process. The process begins, as in planning, with clearly defined and measurable results. Ongoing monitoring of the implementation process is conducted throughout the implementation phase.

The basic idea behind continuous improvement is that if we know the results to be achieved and develop a plan consisting of action steps and measures, and if we watch what occurs when the plan is implemented, then it is possible to identify problems in a timely fashion and take corrective action

Figure 8.3   Continuous Improvement

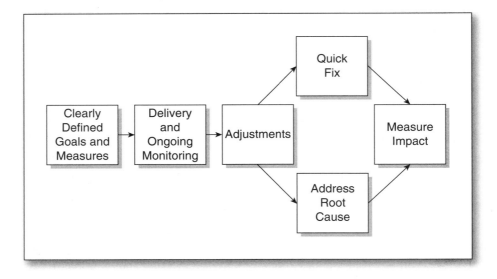

to resolve it. It is only because there is a clear sense of what is expected (requirements for success) that school counselors can look at current practices, identify problems and take corrective action. Continuous improvement principles should be consistently applied to all CBA activities.

Two primary types of adjustments are identified in the figure: quick fixes and root causes. Quick fixes are needed to address emerging needs and get them resolved so as to not disrupt the efficient flow of the process. Root causes, on the other hand, are more systemic in nature and take a longer time to understand and address. Many times the cause of problems requiring quick fixes are due to root causes that keep reoccurring. A two-fold approach, including both quick fixes and root causes, is needed to ensure the least disruptive implementation of the plan.

FOUR TYPES OF PLANS

The planning process requires clearly defined results to be achieved, the action steps needed to achieve them and the measures that will demonstrate progress toward, and achievement of, the specified results. Well-developed front-end plans help sustain a constant focus on the results to be achieved, the steps to be taken and the timetable for when specific actions need to be successfully completed. It reduces the risk of critical tasks not being completed on time or at all. Effective planning also helps maintain a focus on how implementation of the plan is progressing so that corrective action can be applied, as needed. There is no continuous improvement without a self-correcting planning process.

Strategic Plans

Strategic plans are developed at the district level and articulate the vision and strategic direction of the school counseling program. They define what the program seeks to achieve through clearly defined and measurable results statements. Strategic plans are generally for at least a three-year period and establish the long-term future direction for the program. The strategic plan should be aligned with the district's plan and state educational requirements.

A sample CBA school counseling strategic plan is provided in the Construction Zone at the end of this chapter.

Annual Implementation Plans

An annual implementation plan is a more detailed plan that contains specific action steps that will be taken during the current or upcoming school year. Whereas the strategic plan provides a longer view into the future, the implementation plan addresses what should happen within a specific school year. In addition to the action steps, measures that will determine progress toward the results are also identified, along with dates for when specific action steps should be started and completed. Ideally, an annual implementation plan is developed and approved prior to the first day of the school year for which it is being developed. In this way, the plan can be used to guide the implementation of the action steps from the beginning of the year and will help ensure that required actions are not missed.

It is critical to the future of professional K–12 school counseling that it is fully represented in the school/district's strategic and annual planning process. Simply stated, it takes money to run programs. Counseling needs are identified and funds allocated through the planning process.

Counselor-Supervisor Agreements

A third type of plan is a counselor-supervisor agreement. This plan is developed collaboratively by the school counselor(s) and the building principal. It is designed to ensure that the counselor and building administration have achieved consensus on the role and responsibilities of the school counselors and how their performance will be assessed. This plan also gives counselors a way to inform the principal of what they are doing and the contribution they are making to student achievement and the school community.

Individual Counselor Plan for Results

Individual counselors should also develop a personal plan for what they hope to achieve during the school year. Their plans should be aligned with what is stated in the counselor-supervisor agreement, the school-based implementation plan and the district's strategic plan.

CONNECTING CHAPTER 8 TO TOOLKIT CONSTRUCTION SITE 4

Chapter 8 focuses on the need to plan: set goals, develop action steps, implement the plan, monitor progress and evaluate its success based on pre-defined results. A CBA requires well-developed plans at both the organizational and personal levels. A complete planning cycle for school counseling is proposed to ensure that plans are successfully developed and implemented.

Construction Site 4 ("Strategic, Annual and Personal Planning") is designed to help you get started on developing/enhancing an effective planning process for your school counseling program.

As a result of completing Construction Site 4 tasks, you can expect to learn and do the following:

✓ Learn about a complete planning cycle for school counseling.

✓ Learn how to use planning templates to produce four types of plans: a) a three-year strategic plan, b) annual implementation plans, c) counselor-supervisor agreements and d) a personal plan to achieve results.

✓ Review a sample strategic plan for school counseling.

Looking forward to working with you at Toolkit Construction Site 4!

EXAMPLE 8-A

Sample CBA Strategic Plan

— The table below identifies the critical areas, along with the expected results (goals) for each area. The critical areas are organized into three groups: a) program quality, b) organizational effectiveness and c) support for school counseling. An action plan is written for each result.

Group	Critical Area	Expected Results
Program Quality	Counseling, Teaching & Learning	The department's *Framework for School Counseling* clearly delineates the comprehensive school counseling program.
		The Individual Learning Plans program is implemented for all middle and high school students.
		The counseling role in advisories is developed and implemented.
		The counseling curriculum scope and sequence is standardized, where possible.
		Spiraling rubrics for use with counseling activities are developed and implemented.
		A K–12 career development strand is implemented.
		Opportunities for collaborative efforts among counselors and teachers are expanded.
		Repositories of counseling curriculum are posted on the district website.
	Professional Development	A professional development calendar is published annually.
		Professional development modules that target counselor-defined training needs are developed and delivered.
		Support staff is trained in the use of the appropriate tools.
		An increasing number of counselors obtain National Board Counselor Certification.

(Continued)

(Continued)

Group	Critical Area	Expected Results
Organizational Effectiveness	Technology	Use of technology by students in exploring and selecting post-secondary opportunities is expanded.
		Student use of technology for gathering information on post-secondary options (e.g., colleges, careers) is expanded.
	Planning	Strategic and annual planning process is continued.
		Annual implementation plans for upcoming school years are developed.
		Strategic plan is reviewed and updated annually.
	Organizational Support	Key documentation is maintained (keep evergreen).
		A Unified Support Model integrating social work, school psychology and special education is implemented.
		An Advisory Board for School Counseling is established.
	Information Systems/Data	The impact of implementing a comprehensive school counseling program is evaluated.
		A district-wide School Counseling Data Management System is implemented.
		The district produces an annual School Counseling Report Card.
		Meaningful data on the impact of school counseling on the district's personalization efforts are gathered and reported.
	Human Resources	School counseling positions are an interview position.
	Facilities	Facilities provide an environment that is conducive to effective counseling.

Group	Critical Area	Expected Results
Support for School Counseling	School Culture	The quality of the school culture is expanded through a focus on personalized learning environments for students.
	Communications/ Public Relations	Use of electronic communication is expanded among counselors.
		A quarterly newsletter for counselors is published.
	Parent Involvement	Parents are further involved in their child's education through the Individual Learning Plan program
	Partnerships	Strategic partnerships are developed/expanded.

9 CBA Program Implementation

Focus on Delivery

Scenario 1

School counselors in the Forestside School District developed their comprehensive school counseling program based on the ASCA National Model. They purchased an evidence-based commercial product to include in their curriculum. They taught lessons throughout the year in all grades and held small groups as needed to meet student needs. They collected data on their program and were content that it was successful. In September, two new school counselors who were recent graduates of the local university's school counseling program were hired for the middle school. They enthusiastically described the Construct-Based Approach (CBA) to school counseling programs that they had studied in their program and asked if they could help integrate it into the existing program. The veteran counselors listened with interest to their new colleagues but tactfully explained that their program was fine just as it was.

Scenario 2

Two new school counselors were hired in the Forestside School District to expand the program at the middle school. They were both recent graduates of the local university's school counseling program and enthusiastic about the CBA to school counseling programs that they had studied. During the Orientation Day meeting with their new supervisor and colleagues, they shared the research that backed the construct-based approach that explained how knowledge of these constructs was shown to support improvement of student learning and achievement. The supervisor and veteran counselors, who were very proud of their existing program, were intrigued by this new information and after some discussion decided that it would be worth taking the time to investigate further so that they might improve their impact on student achievement. They spent the first half of the school year reviewing schoolwide data and data results from previous lessons taught. Based on the data review, they developed some new curriculum and documented other lessons they had previously taught. They piloted the program for the second semester in the seventh grade and were quite pleased with their results. The supervisor was able to find grant money to pay the counselors for work in the summer to develop curriculum lessons for all grades based on the constructs.

Reflections

Many school counselors currently are implementing strong programs in support of student excellence. Focusing on data-based decision making and integrating the construct-based approach to an existing program can enhance the school counseling program because it focuses on motivation, self-direction, self-knowledge and relationships as four key aspects of student learning.

DELIVERING A CBA PROGRAM WITH FIDELITY

Fidelity means, in part, that the program delivery is consistent and reliable and can be trusted to produce positive results. Creating and sustaining the delivery of a CBA program with fidelity has certain operational requirements that must be in place. This chapter will discuss some of the key requirements for successfully implementing a CBA program: a) roles and accountabilities, b) policies and protocols, c) fluid communication, d) data management and e) professional development. A brief description of each is provided, with a more extensive discussion of CBA school counseling data and its importance in implementing a CBA with fidelity.

See the Construction Zone at the end of this chapter for a list of tools in the *CBA Toolkit* that can be used in conjunction with this chapter.

Roles and Accountabilities

School counselor role statements define the essential functions performed by counselors in the district. They provide a look into what members of the school community can expect as results from having counselors in the schools. The role statement helps define the job responsibilities for which counselors are accountable, identify critical counseling functions and communicate/promote the counselors' role to others in the school community with whom they have direct contact (e.g., students, teachers, parents).

Example 9-A at the end of this chapter provides a sample role statement for school counselors.

Policies and Protocols

Policies are the rules that define what can and cannot be done within the educational community. They are typically generated by legislation (e.g., No Child Left Behind), regulations from state departments of education or a district school board policy.

It is important in a CBA that these policies are documented and are easily accessible to members of the school community. In addition to gathering relevant policies so as to ensure that the CBA program is designed to meet them, it is also important to develop and document the protocols for completing specific functions.

For example, a school district is going to have a grading policy. In this case, the policy adopted by the school board would be documented along with all the steps required in assigning, processing and reporting of grades, including primary responsibility for each action and a timeframe within which the action step should be completed.

Example 9-B at the end of this chapter provides a sample document policy with accompanying protocols.

Fluid Communication

A CBA requires a fluid communication network that produces and distributes vital information in a timely fashion to those who need it to make informed decisions. It is important in a CBA to ensure that information is accurately generated and made available. This requires an understanding of the various audiences in the school community, their informational needs and how they need the information presented so that it is immediately useful.

Professional Development

The CBA is a reframing of the discussion of school counseling student standards, curriculum delivery and student assessments. Research-based constructs and a look at essential school counseling contexts in which all students participate are used to define a new set of student standards. Because the CBA is a new way of looking at school counseling programs, professional development is central to its successful implementation.

Professional development must be ongoing, substantive, meaningful and be conducted in the context of building a community of dialog and self-reflection. In a CBA, high-quality educators become so because they have professional development opportunities and have established a pattern of self-initiated professional development.

DATA MANAGEMENT

This chapter will focus mostly on data management as it is the data-related processes which are a driving force in a CBA. Data are used to assess student proficiency and achievement (see Chapter 7) and to evaluate the impact of the CBA program (see Chapter 10). Establishing a systematic approach to gathering, analyzing and reporting data is an expected result in a CBA. This section will discuss some important considerations when establishing a school counseling data management system.

Data-Based Decision Making

Data-based decision making (DBDM) is a foundational process in a CBA as it provides a systematic approach to using data to make informed decisions regarding the school counseling program and individual student learning processes. It helps establish need, identify appropriate responses and evaluate the impact of the selected interventions.

IDEAS is a five-stage data-based decision-making model delineated by Poynton and Carey (2006). The IDEAS acronym is derived from the first letters of each stage: Identify a Question, Develop a Plan, Execute Plan, Answer Question and Share Results. The model provides a framework for effectively using data to design, deliver and evaluate school counseling programs. This model emphasizes the need to develop and execute plans that are focused on answering specific questions about the school counseling environment.

A CBA is data rich and follows the principles of data-based decision making that focus on establishing student needs, determining appropriate interventions, and assessing the impact of the CBA on student achievement and success. A data management system needs to be developed that identifies relevant data and then gathers, organizes, analyzes and reports it. The data are used to adjust student learning plans and improve practice.

Data to be collected on the impact of school counseling should be data that can also be used to help the school and district meet its data demands. It is important to always think about data in terms of the impact of the CBA, but also use data to promote the significant contribution school counselors make to student success and well-being.

A CBA uses data in two basic ways: a) to determine student progress and achievement, and adjust student learning plans accordingly, and b) to determine the impact of implementing a CBA on school improvement initiatives and the quality of the school community.

Data are used to promote the significant difference school counselors make in student lives. Two of the most important uses of data involve a) providing immediate feedback to students on their performance, reinforcing strengths and working to resolve deficiencies, and b) providing construct-based progress indicators in a section on the report card for meta-cognitive and behavioral assessments.

Another aspect of data to pursue when implementing a CBA is to look at the data the school and district are required to submit (e.g., to state departments of education). School counselors should determine how what they are doing in a CBA contributes to the school and district meeting their data requirements.

Uses of Data in a CBA

Data in a CBA are defined as measureable information about the school counseling program that can be used to design and deliver a quality program, support student development and achievement, and analyze its impact (the extent to which the program achieves its expected results).

The importance and uses of student data were discussed in Chapter 7. School counseling program data also provides valuable information to shape program design and delivery, and improve counselor practice. Data increases counselor capacity to identify and effectively address student need. Data are also important in demonstrating the actual impact of delivering the school counseling program and promoting the value of school counseling to student achievement and the quality of the school community.

> Generally speaking, data can be used in two ways; school counselors can use data to guide program development, and data can be used to evaluate program effectiveness. Practically speaking, using data to guide decision making and using data to provide accountability information go hand in hand. . . . The use of data has become a cornerstone of effective school counseling practice because it allows counselors to identify areas in need of attention and then evaluate the effects of the remedy. (Poynton & Carey, 2006)

The need for factual, measureable school counseling data cannot be overemphasized. There are still far too many people outside the counseling department who do not understand what counselors do and the contributions they make. Many who influence program and budget decisions have negative perceptions about school counselors from when they were in school. Data provides a way to promote school counseling by providing compelling evidence that what school counselors do has a positive impact on both student success and school improvement.

The CBA proposed in this book provides an opportunity to step back and explore how your program is organized in terms of CBA components (student results, counseling curriculum, student assessment) and the effectiveness of your delivery system. Data are an essential part of the implementation process as they are used to make and act on decisions in a timely fashion.

Three Types of Data

Three primary types of data are collected in the four areas: process, perception and results data. The most important data are results data as they provide compelling evidence of the difference the school counseling program makes in student lives. The three types of data can be triangulated to produce a profile of the quality and comprehensiveness of the program and its impact.

Process Data

Process data only provides information on what happened (e.g., number of workshops, number of students attending). It does not provide information on how well the activity was conducted or if expected outcomes were achieved. Process data are important in demonstrating the amount and distribution of effort in implementing the school counseling program.

In addition to process data that can be retrieved through the district's student information system, process data can be gathered through logs. Three logs which help gather process data are as follows:

- Curriculum Delivery Log—gathers data on delivering the CBA curriculum (e.g., number of activities delivered, by and to who, duration of class/workshop, name of activity). These data are used to demonstrate that the core CBA program has been delivered to all students, thus fulfilling a key CBA principle that a curriculum of activities will be provided to all students because of their potential to help students achieve in school and succeed in life. This log allows counselors to know how much of the core CBA curriculum has been delivered and the results as represented in completed artifacts that demonstrate levels of proficiency. Students cannot meet school counseling student standards and competencies without learning what is expected and how to meet the expectation. This log helps ensure that counselors are fulfilling the mission of school counseling to serve all students equally.

- Program Implementation Log—gathers data about the noncurricular steps taken to implement the CBA program. School counselors, like all educators, have more work to accomplish than can be achieved in a normal school day. Prioritization is a required skill when trying to balance the work day. This log can help determine how much time and effort have been expended on both counseling and noncounseling activities. When used in conjunction with the curriculum delivery log, counselors can get a good sense of how their work and time is allocated.

– Student Participation and Artifact Log—data about student participation in the CBA program and completion of artifacts required by the program to establish proficiency. Given the importance of students participating in the learning opportunities and the equally important student results (e.g., completion of artifacts that demonstrate student proficiency), this log captures information on both student participation and artifact completion. Use of the log helps students and adults keep track of where they are in terms of the CBA curriculum and completion of required artifacts.

Perception Data

Perception data provides information regarding what people feel is the impact of the school counseling program on their lives and the school. Student and adult (e.g., counselor, teacher, school leaders, parents) surveys are used to gather participant perceptions.

Results Data

Data provide evidence of actual student work that meets proficiency requirements (students demonstrating what they know and can do as a result of the school counseling program). Results data demonstrate the quality of work being completed and the level of proficiency attained. Short-term results data include assessing the quality of academic and personal plans and the quality of artifacts produced using a rigorous set of acceptance criteria. Long-term results include assessing the impact of the program on schoolwide indicators (e.g., attendance, graduation rates, retention rates, disciplinary referrals).

It is important to consider that perception data can also be results data when the change in perception leads to a change in behavior. For example, in a presurvey 70% of the students were afraid to come to school and in the post-survey only 30% of the students said they were afraid. As a result of school counselor interventions, attendance during the same period increased significantly. Eliminating, or at least learning how to cope with, the fear of coming to school resulted in improved attendance. In this case, the data are both perception and results data.

SCHOOL COUNSELING DATA MANAGEMENT SYSTEM

School counseling, to become data driven, needs to be viewed as a management system and as an integral part of larger educational management systems that use data in a variety of ways, such as for program development and evaluation, school improvement, planning or budgeting. School counselors need a counseling data management system to prove their contribution to student success, their leadership capabilities and their value in school reform. Such a system must be designed, implemented and maintained at the district level and should feed into appropriate state and national data-gathering efforts. A school counseling data management system (SCDMS) provides districts with a systematic approach to becoming data driven.

A SCDMS is required to effectively manage the processes and instruments needed to accomplish these tasks. Designing and implementing a SCDMS can be a daunting task, given all the other data-related activities required in schools. Gathering more and more data is often construed as an add-on that further burdens overworked counselors and takes valuable time away from students. The demands for data to demonstrate accountability are increasing. It is critical that school counselors develop ways to manage data about school counseling. A SCDMS must be systematic and focus on the production of meaningful data (data that can be used to drive decisions). Such an approach must be a central component of the school counseling program.

Expected Results from Implementing a SCDMS

An SCDMS can help you achieve the following as a way of designing and implementing a data management system for school counseling:

– By the beginning of each school year, school counselors produce a data management plan that identifies all data points to be gathered for the school year and documents the protocols for gathering, analyzing and reporting the data. The processes and instruments used for generating and processing the data are ready to be implemented. The data points selected will focus on the following:

+ Linkages to the data (indicators) that districts are required to report. Counselors must show how they impact such data (e.g., attendance, drop-out rates, student achievement, state test scores).

+ Student progress toward standards (e.g., ASCA, National Career Development Guidelines).

+ Impact of implementing the school counseling program.

+ Impact of specific interventions (e.g., anti-bullying program).

The need for data has been a hot topic for many years. For school counseling, we are beginning to see how this need for data is being translated into practice. Research on school counseling has become a national priority. Evidence-based practice is an evolving focus for our profession. In many ways, we are just beginning to figure out what all this means in terms of local districts and schools, from the national to the local level.

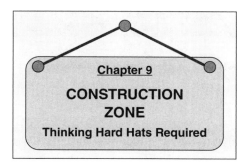

CONNECTING CHAPTER 9 TO TOOLKIT CONSTRUCTION SITE 5

The content of a CBA program has been discussed in the first six chapters of the book. Toolkit Construction Sites 1–3 provided tools to build a CBA to be integrated into your own school counseling program. Chapter 8 and Toolkit Construction Site 4 provided insights into the planning process. For a high-quality program with a well-developed plan to be successfully implemented, some critical organizational areas need to be addressed.

Construction Site 5 ("Program Implementation") provides exercises and templates for addressing key areas related to the successful implementation of a CBA.

As a result of completing Construction Site 5 tasks, you can expect to learn and do the following:

- ✓ Learn about critical organizational support functions that must be operational to successfully implement a CBA (e.g., roles and accountabilities, policies and protocols, a fluid communications network, professional development).

- ✓ Use templates to produced role and accountabilities statements, and policy and protocols documentation.

- ✓ Use a needs assessment tool for determining the professional development needs of those directly involved in delivering the CBA.

- ✓ Use an evaluation tool for determining the impact of the professional development on program quality and counselor performance.

- ✓ Use a tool for developing a plan to produce an "Administrative Handbook for School Counseling" that addresses the operational requirements for implementing a CBA school counseling program.

Looking forward to working with you at Toolkit Construction Site 5!

EXAMPLE 9-A

School Counselor Role Statement

Elementary and Secondary Counselors

Related To	Accountabilities
District	→ Implement the district's Comprehensive School Counseling Program and ensure that students are provided opportunities to achieve the student standards of the American School Counselor Association (ASCA). → Coordinate, monitor and support implementation of the district's Individual Learning Plan (ILP) Program. → Participate in data gathering, analysis and reporting processes.
Teachers and Building Administrators	→ Serve as a resource to faculty (e.g., information sharing). → Consult with teachers regarding individual and classroom behavioral issues, as requested. → Coordinate the interviewing of potential failures when recommended by teachers. → Follow up on referrals from classroom teachers and administrators on truancy cases, as appropriate. → Participate on Evaluation Teams, as needed → Participate on School Crisis Team. → Participate on Teacher Support Teams as a resource, as needed. → Interpret test results and school records for students, parents and other faculty members.
	→ Assist with the administration of testing, as necessary. → Collaborate with classroom teachers on implementation of behavior management plans. → Supervise school counselor interns, if needed.

Related To	Accountabilities
Students	→ Counsel students regarding educational and career planning (e.g., ILP). → Provide classroom instruction in personalization skills (e.g., conflict resolution). → Provide classroom instruction in academic skills (e.g., learning styles, study/test-taking skills). → Assess/counsel students with personal/social issues. → Assess/refer students with personal/social issues to appropriate community agencies, as necessary. → Help to de-escalate emotional situations using counseling skills. → Apply appropriate crisis intervention plan when necessary.
Parents	→ Meet with parents to discuss academic, career and personal/social-related issues. → Meet with parents and assist in referring to community agencies, as needed. → Serve as a resource to parents (e.g., information sharing).
Community Organizations	→ Interface with community agencies. → Refer parents/students to community agencies, as necessary, for services not available in schools.

Additional Secondary Counselor Accountabilities

Related To	Accountabilities
Building Administration	→ Schedule students into classes. → Communicate with teachers about the grading process and timeline.
Students	→ Assist in the application process for high school and private/charter schools. → Write college recommendations for students. → Provide information for college application process (e.g., class rank).

EXAMPLE 9-B

School Counselor Policy and Procedure Documentation

Topic: Counseling Services Referral

Policy:

[School District Policy if appropriate.]

Discussion:

Students are referred for counseling by teacher, administration, parent, self or other student. Students who have behavior problems may be referred for counseling before becoming a discipline problem. If the child has an IEP or is involved with the Evaluation Team, the staff should consult with the Team regarding the behavior problems. The Referral Form is available from the Counseling Office and the school's main office. A standard letter informing parents of services is used by all schools.

Protocols

Who	Action	Form
Counselor	→ Keeps supply of forms in Counseling Office or school's main office. → Communicates location and use of forms to faculty.	Referral Form
Authorized Individual	→ Refers student to school counselor/social worker. Note: Individuals authorized to request a referral include teachers, administrators, nurses, counselors, social workers, parents, self and other students.	Referral Form
Counselor	→ Reviews form and dates it. May require a review of information on form with person who submitted it to get clarification. → Sees student and assesses situation. → Confers with other departments in school, if appropriate (e.g., Special Education or nurse). → Contacts parents. → Maintains a log of students seen, and personal case notes. Do not put notes in the permanent record folder.	Parent Notification Letter

Who	Action	Form
	→ Conducts follow-up with submitter of form and makes recommendations. → Continues counseling, if appropriate. Refers to agency if appropriate, after conferencing with parent. → Give parent contact information for two or more agencies. Traveler's Aid: *RI Directory of Human Services & Government Agencies* is a good source of agency information. → Counselor/social worker may make phone calls to help parents determine if agency can provide services in a timely fashion. → If student is seen for other than academic issue more than three times, complete Medicaid forms (see "Medicaid Reimbursement" located in Section 9 (Forms).	Medicaid Forms

10 CBA Program Implementation

Focus on Evaluation

Scenario 1

Mr. Strong, the principal of Valley High School, entered the school counseling suite with a memo in his hand. Referring to the paper, he announced that the State Commissioner of Education was sending a team of educators to Valley to review their compliance with several state regulations including their comprehensive school counseling program, their attempts to personalize student learning and their Individual Learning Plans (ILPs) for students. Mr. Strong told the counselors that he expected them to be able to lead the response to these regulations when the team arrived in three weeks. He gave them the memo and left the suite with the over-the-shoulder comment, "Don't let me down."

The school counselors did have some documented lessons, but they seldom found the time to actually get into classrooms to teach them. They spent much of their time seeing students individually to review their transcripts and have them discuss goals for their ILPs and plans for post-secondary education. While they had every intention as a department to develop a more comprehensive program, they were so busy with the work they were doing and the duties they were continually being expected to help with, that they never did get very far with their plan. They worked many extra hours in the next three weeks to assemble something that they hoped would pass for a comprehensive program. They developed logs of their meetings with students to demonstrate how they personalized their work with students, including helping them with ILPs. They were hopeful that this would please the team and their principal.

Scenario 2

Mr. Strong, the principal of Valley High School, entered the school counseling suite with a memo in his hand. Referring to the paper, he announced that the State Commissioner of Education was sending a team of educators to Valley to review their compliance with several state regulations including their comprehensive school counseling program, their attempts to personalize student learning and their Individual Learning Plans (ILPs) for students. Mr. Strong told the counselors that he expected them to be able to lead the response to these regulations when the team arrived in three weeks. He gave them the memo and left the suite with the over-the-shoulder comment, "Don't let me down."

The school counselors had spent time during the previous two years developing a comprehensive school counseling program using the construct-based approach. Using the constructs in their curriculum, counselors taught students new knowledge and skills that helped them learn to direct their own lives and benefit maximally from their classroom instruction. They had data that demonstrated the impact on student learning and achievement that they had presented to the faculty recently. The counselors knew that when they explained their approach to implementing this program to the Commissioner's team, it would impress them and please their principal.

Reflections

Embedded assessments in school counseling curriculum can demonstrate student learning. Collecting data on program implementation offers important feedback on the impact of the program. It is important that school counselors maintain an ongoing focus on determining what works and what does not work in the implementation of their school counseling program.

PROGRAM EVALUATION IS AN IMPROVEMENT PROCESS

Construct-Based Approach (CBA) program evaluation is a process of determining the efficacy and impact of delivering a CBA on student learning and the quality of the school community. The evaluation focuses on the specific program being delivered in the school and district. Only by understanding what is working in terms of the local context, and what needs to be improved or fixed, can sustainable change occur. Program evaluations are an opportunity to gather input from all major constituent groups impacting and impacted by the school counseling program (e.g., school counselors, students, other professional support staff, teachers, parents). The quality of the program depends on each constituent group making its contribution to student success. Program evaluation enables all groups to self-assess and listen to the critique of others in determining the current status of the program and the next steps to take.

WHAT NEEDS TO BE EVALUATED

It is important to have a clear understanding of what data are required to accurately evaluate the program, where that data can be found and how the data will be gathered, analyzed and reported. Figure 10.1 identifies six critical areas on which to focus when evaluating a CBA school counseling program.

These areas are critical to the successful implementation of a CBA and can yield valuable information about the status of the program in terms of whether or not

- Planning for the program is effective.

- Delivery of the curriculum and assessment of students produces positive learning outcomes.

- Data gathering, analysis and reporting is well-managed and used to establish need, select appropriate actions and evaluate the impact of the actions.

Figure 10.1 What to Evaluate in a CBA Program

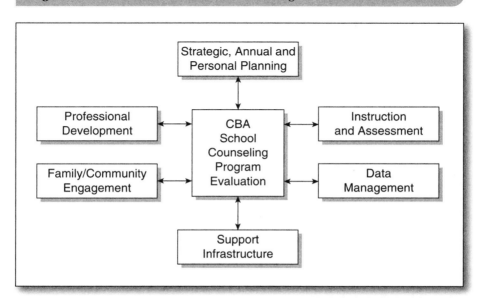

- The CBA support infrastructure is operating efficiently and has well-defined roles and accountabilities, policies and protocol, and a fluid communication.

- Program outreach is evident in terms of increasing parent and family involvement and building partnerships with community organizations, businesses and higher education.

- Professional development opportunities are having a significant impact on improving the CBA program and professional school counselor practice.

Collectively, the information generated in each of the six areas will provide a comprehensive view of the current status of the program and enable school counselors to determine what needs to be improved and how it can be accomplished. A brief description of each critical planning area is provided below.

Strategic, Annual and Personal Planning for Results

Chapter 8 discussed the importance of planning and how four types of plans are used in a CBA (strategic plan, annual implementation plans, counselor-supervisor agreements and personal plan for achieving results).

A complete planning cycle is conducted wherein school counselors define results to be achieved, develop an action plan and identify the measures by which progress toward, and achievement of, the expected results can be determined. It is important to look at the expected results in the plans and apply the accompanying measures to determine progress that has been made. The results of this analysis are used to update current and/or create new plans.

CBA program evaluation in this area seeks to determine how effective the planning processes have been. Critical questions can include the following: Were the results well-defined? Was the action plan reasonable and achievable? Were the school counselors good stewards to the plan? Were the measures specified in the plan gathering the most relevant data?

Instruction and Assessment

With the expectation that students will meet school counseling student standards and competencies, a CBA needs to deliver a rigorous school counseling curriculum that provides students with opportunities to learn, apply and demonstrate what they know and can do. The standards of student excellence form the basis (learning targets) of the curriculum activities.

The school counseling curriculum is results based. Students are expected to acquire relevant knowledge, develop appropriate skills, and embrace attitudes, behaviors and habits of mind that lead to personal fulfillment and future success. The core set of CBA curriculum activities (those intended for delivery to all students) provides students with optimal opportunities to learn and have their progress toward the results assessed.

A CBA curriculum has embedded assessments in its activities that are tied to the construct-based competencies on which the activity is based. This allows school counselors to gather data about the impact of their interactions with students and provide immediate feedback to students and others and make adjustments to the learning plan in a timely fashion.

CBA program evaluation examines the impact of delivering the program and the extent to which students progress toward or achieved the results. The various student assessment results are analyzed to determine if students actually increased their knowledge, developed their skills (applying knowledge in authentic contexts), and embraced appropriate attitudes, behaviors and habits of mind. Strong evidence of differences the CBA program has made in student lives can, in part, be attributed to the successful delivery of the CBA content and accurate assessments of student performance. Lack of evidence of any difference the CBA has made in student lives points to possible causes for students not learning in the instruction and assessment processes.

Data Management

A CBA is data rich and follows the principles of data-based decision making that focus on establishing student needs, determining appropriate interventions and assessing the impact of the CBA on student achievement and school quality. A data management system needs to be developed (see Chapter 9) that identifies relevant data and then gathers, organizes, analyzes and reports that data. The data are used to adjust student learning plans, and improve both program quality and professional school counselor practice.

Data to be collected on the impact of school counseling should include data elements that can also be used to help the school and district meet its data demands. It is important to always think about data in terms of the impact of the CBA, but also use that data to promote the significant contribution school counselors make to student success and well-being.

A CBA uses data in two basic ways: a) determine student progress and achievement and adjust student learning plans accordingly, and b) determine the impact of implementing a CBA on school improvement initiatives and the quality of the school community.

Data are used to promote the significant difference school counselors make in student lives. Two of the most important uses of data involve a) providing immediate feedback to students on their performance, reinforcing strengths and working to resolve deficiencies, and b) providing construct-based progress indicators in a section on the report card for metacognitive and behavioral assessments.

Another aspect of data to pursue when implementing a CBA is to look at the data the school and district are required to submit (e.g., to state departments of education). School counselors should determine how what they are doing in a CBA contributes to the school and district meeting their data requirements.

CBA program evaluation analyzes the data on student learning plus it closely examines the data-related processes and whether they were well-organized and well-managed and, in the final analysis, generated the data that were necessary to complete an accurate program evaluation.

Relevant evaluation questions might include: Does the data show differences in students' knowledge, skills, attitudes and behaviors? Did the data make a difference in identifying students' needs, selecting appropriate interventions and evaluating results? What did you learn from the data? How was the data used to make improvements and effect change?

Support Infrastructure

Organizational support involves roles and accountabilities, clearly defined policies and protocols, and a fluid communication network that produces and distributes vital information in a timely fashion to those who need it to make informed decisions.

Organizational support addresses the operational requirements for implementing a CBA. An important step school counselors can take in implementing a CBA is to develop, or enhance, the district's documented role and accountabilities statement. Likewise, another important step is to develop clear policy and protocols, standardizing them when appropriate. A third step is to identify the informational needs of the various constituent groups in the school community and determine the best way to ensure everyone is informed.

Program evaluation questions that are relevant to this area can include: Is the school counselor role clearly understood by counselors and other members of the school community, or is there ambiguity and confusion regarding the counselor's role? Have critical policies and processes been documented with established protocols that standardize processes and forms, where appropriate? Is vital information generated in a timely fashion and disseminated to those who need it?

Family and Community Engagement

Program outreach efforts are critical to the successful implementation of a CBA. School counselors can engage parents and increase parental involvement in their children's education. Likewise, school counselors can establish and sustain meaningful partnerships with the community at large to help support the delivery of the CBA and achievement of its results.

Professional Development

Initiatives to redefine knowledge and skill requirements require a shift in how school counselors understand student learning needs. Just as it is the responsibility of counselors and teachers to provide students with opportunities to learn the new knowledge and develop/enhance their skills, so too it is the responsibility of educational institutions and agencies to provide adequate training in how to deliver the CBA learning opportunities.

Professional development must be ongoing, substantive, meaningful and be conducted in the context of building a community of dialog and self-reflection. High-quality educators become so because they have professional development opportunities and have established a pattern of self-initiated professional development.

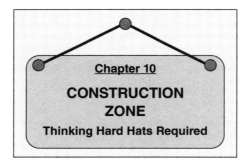

CONNECTING CHAPTER 10 TO TOOLKIT CONSTRUCTION SITE 6

Compelling evidence is needed that demonstrates the significant contribution of school counselors and school counseling programs to student success and school improvement. Data are required to accurately determine the impact of implementing a CBA.

Construction Site 6 ("Evaluating CBA Program Efficacy and Impact") is designed to help you view program evaluation from the perspective of a CBA.

As a result of completing Construction Site 6 tasks, you can expect to learn and do the following:

✓ Learn about evaluating the fidelity and efficacy of a CBA.

✓ Use a CBA evaluation instrument to determine the impact of the program.

✓ Conduct a survey to determine the impact of the CBA from various constituent groups.

✓ Produce an annual accountability report on your school counseling program.

Looking forward to working with you at Toolkit Construction Site 6!

11 CBA's Contribution to School Improvement Initiatives

Scenario 1

The superintendent of Mapleleaf School District was emphatic that every content area and program in the district must show their alignment with the Common Core Standards and 21st Century Skills. Since the state was leaning toward their adoption and the district was trying to position itself for increased state funding, he felt that demonstration of that alignment would work in their favor. When the district's school counselors received the superintendent's memo on this topic, they met to work on the alignment of their program. The Counseling Director had printed copies of the standards and skills for each counselor. They all read the material, and although they saw some common ground, they didn't know how to get started with an alignment.

Scenario 2

The school counselors of Mapleleaf School District had developed their program using the Construct-Based Approach (CBA). When they received the memo from the superintendent stating that he was requiring every content area and program to demonstrate an alignment with the Common Core Standards and 21st Century Skills, they felt that it would be a doable task since their construct-based approach had similarities to both of these initiatives. All three initiatives seek to redefine knowledge and skill requirements based on research and evidence-based practice. They include student standards curriculum, instruction, student assessment, professional development, environment and data. The counselors divided up the sections of the task and all set to work on their alignment.

Reflections

The CBA offers research on the educational impact of the school counseling program to student achievement. Finding commonalities with statewide and district-wide initiatives can help demonstrate the value that a CBA to the school counseling program has on the holistic education of every student.

Chapters 8–10 provided a glimpse into what is required to successfully implement a CBA school counseling program. This chapter addresses the need for a CBA to be integrated with and contribute to other school improvement initiatives in the district. The contribution of a CBA to current practice (ASCA National Model, Evidence-Based Practice) is discussed, along with the contribution of a CBA to national knowledge and skill requirements initiatives (Common Core, Partnership for 21st Century Skills, ACT) and the contribution of a CBA to learning and behavior intervention initiatives (Response to Intervention, Positive Behavioral Intervention System, Early Warning Indicators).

CONTRIBUTION TO CURRENT PRACTICE

Two major influences on school counseling programs and counselor practice are the American School Counselor Association's "ASCA National Model" (2012) and the work being done in evidence-based school counseling practice.

ASCA National Model

The primary points of intersection between the construct-based approach and the ASCA National Model are student standards, use of a challenging curriculum and student assessments. The most recent version of the ASCA Model (2012) encourages school counselors to consider district and state initiatives to inform their program and align with the ASCA Student Standards.

The proposed construct-based approach is grounded in a review of more than 50 years of research, including available research from 2013. This is in contrast to the ASCA student standards, which were first developed by Campbell and Dahir (1997). There have been major advances in research regarding our increasing understanding of how the brain functions, how students learn and what are the most effective strategies for delivering a standards-based school counseling program focused on student achievement, excellence and well-being.

In addition, the ASCA Model states that school counselors "use the standards to assess student growth and development, guide the development of strategies and activities and create a program that helps students achieve their highest potential" (ASCA, 2012).

Evidence-Based Practice

Evidence-based practice is a movement that originated in the field of medicine and is now widely accepted as a model for guiding practice in a wide range of human service fields including, for example, public health (Bronson, Gurney, & Land, 1999), nursing (Deaton, 2001), school psychology (Kratochwill & Shernoff, 2003) and counseling psychology (Chwalisz, 2003). Sexton, Schofield and Whiston (1997) argued for the school counseling profession's adoption of evidence-based practice and have indicated how adopting such an approach would lead to more effective practice, greater coherence between training and practice, and a clearer connection between practice and student outcomes.

Evidence-based practice has been defined as "the integration of the best evidence with clinical experience and patient values" (Sackett, Straus, Richardson, Rosenberg, & Hayes, 2000, p. 1). Dimmitt, Carey and Hatch (2007) have developed a three-domain model of evidence-based practice in school counseling. They suggest that professional decisions concerning school counseling interventions should be made with reference to evidence related to problem description, outcome research and intervention evaluation. These three areas reflect knowing what problems need to be addressed, knowing what is likely to work and knowing that an intervention made a positive difference for students. Problem description evidence is drawn from school data mining and the intentional collection of needs assessment data. The outcome research literature is the primary source for evidence that a given intervention is likely to achieve positive results. School counselors' evaluation of interventions that they have implemented is the primary source for information on whether or not a given intervention has had its desired effect on students, learning and behavior change. For Dimmitt et al. (2007) being engaged in evidence-based practice means that a school counselor is basing professional decisions on these three sources of evidence.

The construct-based approach to student standards is a natural complement to evidence-based school counseling practice. By using a construct-based approach, school counselors will ensure that the learning standards upon which their program is based are tightly aligned with aspects of student motivation, self-knowledge, self-direction and relationship skills that have been established through research to be both: 1) critically important in terms of students' academic achievement, success, and well-being; and 2) able to be enhanced by educational interventions (see Chapter 3). School counselors will know that their interventions are aimed at the right targets.

Because the constructs provide a more focused description of desired student abilities, school counselors will also find it much easier to either select standardized curriculum-based programs or construct effective curriculum units.

CONTRIBUTION TO KNOWLEDGE AND SKILL REQUIREMENT INITIATIVES

Every profession defines its standards of excellence. For students, these standards of excellence are articulated in standard and competency statements (see Chapter 5) and serve as the focal point of CBA school counseling curriculum activities. They also form the basis for determining student proficiency and achievement. This section shows that the CBA is doing for school counseling what Common Core State Standards (CCSS) are doing for math and English language arts (ELA), and Partnership for 21st Century Skills (P21) is doing for life and employability skills.

Common Core State Standards

This book is a reframing of the discussion on school counseling student standards, challenging curriculum and student assessments. A defining characteristic of a reframing effort is that knowledge and skill requirements are redefined in terms of the present and currently perceived needs for the future. In short, knowledge and skill requirements can, over time, become outdated and in need of revision.

The standards movement has been a driving force in redefining education, its priorities and its challenges. Two current national reframing initiatives discussed in this section are the Common Core State Standards (CCSS) Initiative and the Partnership for 21st Century Skills (P21) Initiative. Like the CBA proposed in this book, CCSS and P21 have reviewed the current and future requirements for success. The CBA proposes a new set of school counseling student standards, a construct-based curriculum, and student assessments that can be used to monitor and report student progress.

The CCSS Initiative is led by the nation's governors and education commissioners. The intent of the CCSS is to define clear expectations (knowledge and skill requirements) that are aligned with what colleges expect and employers require for entry-level positions (National Governors Association Center for Best Practices, Council of Chief State School Officers, 2010).

CCSS hopes to achieve a single set of standards for ELA and math that everyone uses and can lead to students graduating from high school prepared to successfully enter the post-secondary world. The move to reexamine knowledge and skill requirements is generally motivated by a perceived inadequacy of the current knowledge and skill sets. The knowledge and skills required in an information age are far different from those required in the industrial age, where many of our current educational constructs were first designed and implemented.

The CCSS chose ELA and math because of their importance to student learning and student achievement. For these core subjects, they have defined a new set of standards and competencies that are more relevant to the present and to planning for the future, and can serve as challenging learning targets for students.

CCSS has a primary focus on academic content and students being able to learn the content and demonstrate their learning by taking high-stakes tests and other forms of assessment that measure the acquisition and use of knowledge. It also recognizes the need to focus on skill development as an integral part of cognitive development.

CBA and CCSS Skills Alignment

One way for school counselors to figure out how two initiatives interact is to identify skills that are being developed by each initiative. The CBA and CCSS have a shared focus on helping students develop some critical skills. In order for the CBA to make a contribution to other initiatives, and find support for the CBA from others, school counselors should be able to identify the points of intersection where goals common to both initiatives can be achieved through shared experience. These are the types of connections that integrate the insights, experiences and creativity for in-depth dialog and productivity.

Partnership for 21st Century Skills

The Partnership for 21st Century Skills (P21) is another national initiative that is redefining what knowledge and skills are required for success in school, work and life. Just as the Common Core initiative acknowledges the importance of both cognitive and social skill development, P21 considers a broad spectrum of factors influencing student learning in developing its skill set.

To succeed in the 21st century, all students will need to perform to high standards and acquire mastery of rigorous core subject material. All students also will need to gain the cognitive and social skills that enable them to deal with the complex challenges of our age. Readiness emphasizes life and career skills, learning and innovation skills, information, media and technology skills as well as core subjects and 21st century themes. The P21 initiative "addresses both the core academic knowledge and the complex thinking skills that are required for success in college, life and career in the 21st century" (Partnership for 21st Century Skills, 2011, p. 4).

P21 is committed to looking at a wide range of factors influencing student learning to develop its skill sets, including both cognitive and metacognitive processes. Skill is the ability to do and do it well. Skill development is a process of applying knowledge (what is known) to tasks that need to be completed. Students learn from each experience and are continuously modifying their way of looking at and responding in the world. A school counselor's commitment to helping students develop their learning skills opens a door to their future.

From the perspective of a CBA, school counselors are helping students understand how they learn in terms of their motivation, self-direction, self-knowledge and relationships. A CBA uses the school counseling curriculum to provide learning opportunities for all students in which they can acquire knowledge such as facts and concepts and are given opportunities to apply what they are learning in authentic contexts (skill development).

Assessing student progress and achievement is ongoing. Curriculum activities have embedded assessments to provide immediate feedback to students. A construct-based portion of the school's report card contains a teacher-rated scale focused on students' metacognitive skill development and behavior patterns.

P21 offers an extensive list of 21st century skills organized under numerous headings. Just as we wanted to find common ground between CBA and the CCSS above, we can use the same process by identifying P21 skills to which CBA standards and competencies are particularly relevant.

Here are some examples of the skill statements that we have grouped under the four constructs: motivation, self-direction, self-knowledge and relationships. Table 11.1 shows the relevance of the selected skills to a particular construct.

As is evident in the following table, there are multiple skills addressed by the P21 initiative to which school counselors can contribute through a CBA. For example, under the motivation construct, P21 identifies a commitment to lifelong learning and a desire to excel beyond minimum proficiency requirements as needed for success in the 21st century. One of the unique features of school counseling is helping students learn how to learn and become successful lifelong learners.

ACT'S FIVE PRINCIPLES

This section discusses the alignment of CBA student assessments with ACT's principles/standards that delineate five principles to inform "designing assessment and accountability systems that use growth models for the

Table 11.1 Examples of Skill Statements Linked to Constructs

Motivation	Relationships
→ Demonstrate commitment to learning as a lifelong process → Go beyond basic mastery of skills and/or curriculum to explore and expand one's own learning and opportunities to gain expertise → Be accountable for results	→ Demonstrate ability to work effectively and respectfully with diverse teams → Assume shared responsibility for collaborative work, and value the individual contributions made by each team member → Conduct themselves in a respectable, professional manner → Respect cultural differences and work effectively with people from a range of social and cultural backgrounds → Respect and appreciate team diversity → Act responsibly with the interests of the larger community in mind → 21st century standards, assessments, curriculum, instruction, professional development and learning environments must be aligned to produce a support system that produces 21st century outcomes for today's students.
Self-Direction	
→ Reason effectively → Set and meet goals, even in the face of obstacles and competing pressures → Set goals with tangible and intangible success criteria	
Self-Knowledge	
→ Reflect critically on learning experiences and processes → Reflect critically on past experiences in order to inform future progress	

purpose of improving the college and career readiness of high school graduates" (ACT, 2012, p. 1). Table 11.2 displays the five principles.

CBA Alignment with ACT's Five Principles

Accountability is essential to a fully operational educational environment that is responsive to students' development needs. A construct-based approach to school counseling is aligned with ACT's five principles and provides structured processes and tools for establishing school counselor accountability through its program implementation processes (planning, delivery, evaluation). Some thoughts on ways in which a CBA is aligned with each of the principles are provided below.

Table 11.2 ACT's Five Principles

1.	The *minimum goal* for every student should be to become college and career ready by high school graduation.
2.	College and career readiness should be monitored as early as possible and communicated to students, parents and educators so that they know whether students are on track and can tailor instructional strategies as needed.
3.	The assessment of school performance should be based on multiple measures, including overall student growth and growth for student subgroups—including special needs, low-income, underrepresented racial/ethnic minority and limited English proficient students.
4.	Growth modeling results should be used to better understand strengths and weaknesses in a school's curriculum and practices.
5.	The assessment of teacher performance should employ multiple measures, including student growth toward college and career readiness.

Principle 1.

School counselors focus on preparedness from the earliest grades. At the high school level, in particular, the major focus is on helping students meet graduation requirements and successfully navigate the transition from high school to the very different post-secondary world of further education and/or pursuing other options (e.g., finding full-time employment or entering the military). Goal setting and future planning are key components of this process. CBA student assessments play a key role in achieving this goal by pointing out throughout the school year how they are progressing toward the standards and competencies they are expected to achieve.

Principle 2.

A CBA has a built-in monitoring system. The school counseling curriculum is based on the construct-based standard and competency statements. All CBA activities have embedded assessments that are aligned with the standards and competencies and can be used to provide students with immediate feedback on how well they did in learning and applying what was being taught. In addition, a CBA-based component on the student report card provides periodic opportunities to monitor and assess progress throughout the school year.

Principle 3.

The monitoring of student growth is an essential process for which school counselors are well positioned to complete. This is due in large part to the multi-tier approach in a CBA that has school counselors interacting with students at the whole school, whole class, small group and individual basis. These levels of interaction each provide different types of assessments that can be used to determine student need and deliver interventions that produce positive results. All this assessment data can be used to produce an accurate and well-rounded profile of individual, small group and collective needs.

Principle 4.

The CBA curriculum is designed to help students achieve construct-based standards and competencies. Embedded assessments provide valuable information about student learning, but also provide insights into the impact of a particular activity or intervention and how it can be improved.

Principle 5.

College and career readiness is one of the contexts for school counseling programs described in Chapter 4 ("Relevant Contexts for K–12 School Counseling Programs"). Because of the importance of preparing students for both college and careers, and the fact that it is a primary goal for professional school counselors, it could be included in the evaluation process.

CBA CONTRIBUTION TO SCHOOL-BASED INTERVENTION INITIATIVES

"The combination of RTI and PBIS provides effective instructional strategies for both academic and behavior systems" (PBIS.org, n.d.). While starting out in more specialized contexts (e.g., special education), these initiatives are now being promoted for all students with different levels of interventions being used depending on whether it is for a whole class or school, a sub-population of students, or individual students. Efforts to integrate Response to Intervention (RTI) and Positive Behavioral Interventions and Supports (PBIS) significantly broaden the focus of both programs into a more powerful, holistic and systematic approach to determining and addressing student needs with a more rapid and effective responses.

RTI is "the practice of providing high-quality instruction and interventions matched to student need, monitoring progress frequently to make decisions about changes in instruction or goals, and applying child response data to important educational decisions" (Batsche et al., 2005).

PBIS is based on a problem-solving model and aims to prevent inappropriate behavior through teaching and reinforcing appropriate behaviors (U.S. Office of Special Education Programs [OSEP], 2009).

Core Principles Shared by RTI and PBIS

The PBIS website lists six core principles shared by RTI and PBIS. Each of these offers points of potential alignments with the CBA.

First, instruction has to be research based and of high quality. The CBA is research based (see Chapter 3). The CBA student standards, challenging curriculum and student assessments provide high-quality opportunities to learn. In particular, students are expected to learn about themselves (who they are now and want to become), explore how they think and act in the world, learn how to plan for their future, increase their motivation to learn and engage in meaningful relationships that contribute to their growth.

Second, screening must be universal and classroom based. A CBA behavioral component of a report card is an ongoing screening process for identifying student need and arranging for appropriate academic and behavioral interventions. The report is a combination of academic and behavioral results for a specified period of time. Academic grades help determine the level of cognitive development as measured by content standards and state-mandated tests. The construct-based portion of the report card focuses more on the students' ability and desire to learn, incorporating metacognitive skills and environmental influences.

Third, the approach is collaborative and results in team building. This is particularly evident in the role of school counselors in intervention initiatives like RTI, PBIS and Early Warning Indicator and Intervention Systems (EWS). Establishing a construct-based school counseling program is a collaborative, team-building effort. School counselors, other professional support team members, teachers and building leaders (e.g., principal, administrator in charge of school counseling, school improvement team members) all need to be involved in established an environment that is learner centered and promotes a holistic view of students by giving equal weight to both academic and behavioral results. At times, school counselors serve in the role of team leader.

Fourth, individual needs are matched with evidence-based practice. School counselors are very experienced and adept at understanding student need and identifying appropriate strategies and interventions to help them resolve barriers to their learning and fulfill their needs. Comprehensive school counseling programs are need driven. As noted above, they apply a tiered approach consisting of whole class preventative curriculum lessons, targeted small group interventions and individual one-on-one interactions.

Counselor interactions with students are informed by the principles of differentiated instruction wherein counselors define students' need in terms of all students, targeted populations of some students and individual students with the greatest need and who are most at-risk.

Fifth, progress is continuously monitored. The construct-based report card is an important tool for monitoring student progress as it is periodic (e.g., four times a year) and establishes student proficiency in terms of those areas that are strongly related to the role of school counselors. Since school counselors are delivering many of the strategies and interventions recommended by the RTI and PBIS teams, they are a primary source of input and feedback to the team regarding the needs of individual students.

Sixth, parent involvement is key. Counselor-parent interactions are another key component of a construct-based school counseling program. It is a basic principle of the program that parents need to understand the importance of motivation, self-direction, self-knowledge and relationships to learning in general, and how their child is doing in relation to the construct-based assessment categories on the report card. The counselor-parent interaction is ongoing, beginning with teaching parents about the constructs and the assessment being used to assess their child's progress, and followed by assistance in interpreting their child's assessment results, and engaging the parents by helping them to become more proactively involved in their child's learning, school achievement and success in life.

Early Warning Indicators

Many districts are implementing Early Warning Indicator and Intervention Systems (EWS). EWS represent a collaborative approach among educators, administrators, parents and communities to using data effectively to keep students on the pathway to graduation.

The best EWS are characterized by a combination of features that enable rapid identification of students who are in trouble; rapid interventions that are targeted to students' immediate and longer-term need for support, redirection and greater success; the frequent monitoring of the success of interventions; a rapid modification of interventions that are not working; and shared learning from outcomes (Bruce, Bridgeland, Fox, & Balfanz, 2011, p. 2).

EWS are possible because of research on signs of early disengagement that predict dropping out and school information systems that enable schools to track students on these signs. EWS tell us *which* students are becoming disengaged but not *why* they are becoming disengaged. Combining construct-based standards with EWS indicators supplies the missing information that counselors need to find out why students are becoming disengaged and what should be done about it.

When combined with modern school information systems, these indicators allow for the rapid and automatic identification of students as soon as they "trip" the critical value of the indicator associated with disengagement. In schools with EWS, administrators and counselors are automatically notified by the school information system when a student "trips" the indicator. School counselors then are responsible for intervening and helping the student reengage with school.

The CBA can help focus on areas of student development that have significant impact on students. By focusing on motivation, self-direction, self-knowledge and relationships addressed through a preventive school counseling curriculum, there is the potential for shaping and changing thinking and behavior patterns before they become engrained and disruptive to individual, small group and whole class learning. The CBA is readily aligned with other national initiatives that are focused on curricular, organizational and methodological ways to improve the learning and development of students. A CBA adds value to these other initiatives by indicating the critical student learning domains that must be attended to in order to promote the development of engaged learners: their motivation, self-direction, self-knowledge and relationship skills.

TOWARD A MORE
HOLISTIC VIEW OF STUDENT LEARNING

Current literature reveals a growing effort to take a more holistic view of student learning that includes both cognitive and behavioral aspects of how students learn. This is evident in efforts to view Common Core State Standards (CCSS) and the Partnership for 21st Century Skills (P21) collectively to get a much broader basis for understanding the learning needs of the whole child. Likewise, efforts to integrate Response to Intervention (RTI) and Positive Behavior Intervention System (PBIS) have the similar intent of incorporating both the cognitive (academic) and metacognitive (e.g., attitudes, behaviors, habits of mind) when determining and responding to student needs.

Such integration efforts are helping to establish a more holistic view of the complexities of the whole child. This move toward affirming the conceptual equivalence of the cognitive and metacognitive domains will provide school counselors with a richer environment in which to work because the metacognitive processes that they support will be viewed at the same level of importance as knowledge acquisition and cognitive skill development.

One of the outcomes of these integration trends will be a much clearer understanding of how students learn and what school counselors can do to help improve their learning processes. Research and evidence-based practice will produce findings that suggest where and in what ways school counselor efforts have, or potentially can have, the greatest impact. The CBA described in this book is designed according to that principle: using research findings to determine the educational constructs that, when focused on by school counselors, have the greatest positive impact on student achievement and success. Student standards and competencies are then identified for each construct and are used as the foundation (learning targets) for the CBA curriculum. Student assessments are embedded in the curriculum to help determine students' progress toward and achievement of the school counseling student standards.

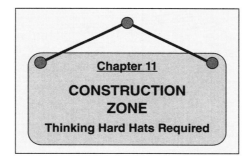

Chapter 11

CONSTRUCTION ZONE

Thinking Hard Hats Required

CONNECTING CHAPTER 11 TO TOOLKIT CONSTRUCTION SITES 4–6

No program can be implemented in isolation. Schools have multiple programs, including school counseling, that all contribute to achieving the goals of the school. Since multiple programs are all trying to effect positive change in the same students, it is sensible for counselors to engage in dialog with members of other initiatives to ensure that the potential contribution of a collaborative effort is fully maximized.

Collaborative opportunities such as those discussed in this chapter can be used in Construction Sites 4–6. CS4 ("Planning") can be used to develop plans for building and sustaining a meaningful collaboration with other school improvement initiatives. CS5 ("Program Delivery") can be used to ensure the cross-initiative roles and accountabilities are clearly-define and essential protocols documented. CS6 ("Program Evaluation") can be used to examine the quality and impact of the collaborative efforts.

As a result of completing Construction Sites 4–6 tasks, you can expect to learn and do the following:

✓ Learn how a CBA relates to other national initiatives:

- Comprehensive school counseling programs (ASCA, Evidence-Based Practice).
- Redefining knowledge and skill requirements (Common Core, Partnership for 21st Century Skills, ACT).
- School-based interventions (RTI, PBIS, EWS).

✓ Learn how collaboration is central to the successful implementation of a CBA.

Looking forward to working with you at Toolkit Construction Site 4!

12 Power and Potential

Scenario 1

When a new superintendent came to Meadowland School District, she set out to make improvements in all areas that affected the improvement of student achievement. She reviewed all programs and areas of instruction and gave feedback to the directors of every department in the district. Her feedback to the Director of School Counseling was that the program seemed weak in its content and recommended that the counselors work on their curriculum and implementation. The school counselors were willing to improve their program, but they were unsure of how to begin. They had lessons developed for every grade level and didn't understand what the superintendent meant when she said they were weak. Not wanting to seem incompetent or contrary, they each took on the task of writing new lessons for their respective grades and hoped she would like them better than the existing ones.

Scenario 2

The school counselors of Meadowland had heard from counselors in her previous district that their new superintendent was very focused on everyone demonstrating how they could impact student achievement. The school counselors felt that with their Construct-Based Approach (CBA) to their school counseling program, they were in a good position to do just that. They decided to be proactive, and they worked as a team to compile a binder of material on the program to present to the superintendent as soon as they were able to arrange a meeting with her. They included the research base of their program, their curriculum scope and sequence, sample lessons from each level and a PowerPoint they had presented to the School Board last June that demonstrated with data the impact they were having on student achievement in each of the levels. They anticipated a good meeting with her.

Reflections

It is critical for school counselors to be able to communicate the essential nature and benefits of a CBA and to help others understand what a successfully implemented CBA looks like in a school. Knowing the value of the CBA to the school counseling program helps the school counselors advocate for their program.

WHAT IS POWER AND POTENTIAL?

Power is the capacity to influence and transform lives—the lives of students, families, school counselors, teachers, administrators and other members of the school community. Power is the capacity to make a difference in students' ability to achieve and succeed. Potential points to what is possible—what can be achieved by investing time and energy and resources toward desired results. The power and potential of a construct-based, context-sensitive school counseling program is that it can transform student lives, counselor practice and program efficacy by creating, expanding and nurturing possibilities for student growth and development. The power and potential of using constructs and contexts as primary filters for designing, delivering and evaluating counseling programs is that school counselors can increasingly make a significant difference in the ways students think and behave in the world.

A VISION TO LIVE BY

In Chapter 5, "A Vision to Live By" was introduced to articulate the primary results students are expected to achieve through participation in a CBA. Helping students become motivated, self-directed, self-knowledgeable and relational learners is a substantive contribution school counselors can make to student achievement and success in school, work and life. See Figure 12.1.

Making a Difference in Student Lives

A primary goal of the school counseling profession is to make a difference in student lives. Imagine the differences that can be made. Students have a better chance of achieving at their highest potential because school counselors are teaching them how to learn, how to plan for their future

Figure 12.1   A Vision to Live By

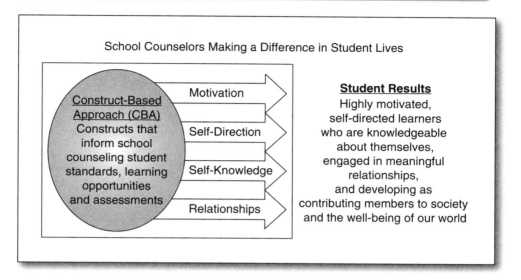

success and how to cope with the myriad challenges they face growing up and maturing into adulthood.

Imagine students benefiting from increased engagement in the learning process and in their relationships with others because school counselors are helping them develop their metacognitive skills that support cognitive achievement. Imagine how much fuller student lives can be because counselors are helping students become motivated to explore and pursue their possible selves and the pathways to get there.

Perhaps the most powerful gift we can offer students is to help them achieve these results and guide them toward becoming the vision of student excellence inherent in a CBA.

SUMMARY OF KEY POINTS

It is our hope that this book will inspire dialog and action that results in the implementation of a construct-based approach to school counseling as a way of improving the quality of school counseling programs and making the counseling program a key contributor to improvements in student achievement and preparedness for the post-secondary world.

The CBA provides a strong research base that focuses school counselors on critical areas of student development in which counselors can make a significant difference. Additionally, the constructs suggested by research are also measurable in terms of student performance.

What School Counselors Do

It is important to understand the central role of school counselors in K–12 educational environments. School counselors help students develop the knowledge, skills, attitudes, beliefs and habits of mind that enable them to profit maximally from their instructional opportunities and experiences. This is in contrast to the primary role of classroom teachers who attend to the more obvious, observable and measureable aspects of achievement. Teachers focus on the facts, concepts and processes that reflect mastery of a particular area of knowledge and enact effective instructional techniques that maximize students' opportunities to acquire knowledge and expertise.

Education of the whole child requires both cognitive and metacognitive skill development. Cognitive development in the current educational systems is primarily within the purview of content area teachers. Metacognitive development is primarily within the purview of school counselors and other professional support staff. It is critical to the successful education of the whole child that school counselors and teachers collaborate to ensure a balanced approach to identifying and meeting the learning needs of every child.

Importance of Research

It is difficult to find any writing on or regulations for school improvement without coming across the terms "research-based" and "evidence-based." The CBA relies heavily on research findings that identify critical types of evidence.

"Research-based" in this book means that the constructs, contexts, standards and competencies were written to reflect student abilities, competencies, capabilities and skills that 1) have been established by research in educational and developmental psychology to be strongly related to students' academic achievement and later success in life, and 2) are acquired or perfected through experience and learning. Lines of research were chosen that connected to student competencies that were primarily within the domain of the work of counselors—that fell within the academic, personal/social and career development domains of school counseling practice.

The school counseling profession must be explicitly grounded in research in terms of how its programs are designed, delivered and evaluated.

Although there is a growing body of research on student development and the impact of school counseling programs, there is still a great need for additional research and evaluation at the higher education level, and action research at the local level, that continuously refine our understanding of student need and determination of those strategies and practices that have the greatest potential for fulfilling that need.

Of particular interest is research being conducted on the impact of meta-cognitive skill development on student success and the economic benefits of providing students with learning opportunities that help them develop and successfully apply noncognitive skills in their learning and lives.

Results-Based Approach

The notion of results as learning targets we want students to achieve and a result as the end of a process in which students participate are critical to the successful implementation of a student-centered school counseling program. Results can be understood as both the planned, measureable outcomes of an effective school counseling program and as the knowledge, attitudes and skills acquired and demonstrated by students as the expected outcomes of the school counseling program.

As noted in Chapter 2, a results-based approach is "designed to guarantee that all students acquire the competencies to become successful in school and to make a successful transition from school to higher education, to employment or to a combination of higher education and work" (Johnson & Johnson, 2003).

Two primary types of results were discussed in Chapter 5: standards (end results that students are expected to achieve by the time they graduate) and competencies (proficiency-building results that students are expected to achieve at various times along the K–12 learning continuum). Standard statements proposed in this book are based on constructs while competency statements are based on contexts that are relevant to student growth and development within the purview of the school counseling program.

Role of Curriculum

The school counseling curriculum is the primary vehicle for delivering a results-based program to students. The curriculum enables us to provide core learning experiences to all students and uniformly assess their progress and levels of achievement. Counseling curriculum activities are aligned with the standards. Competency statements clarify the intent of the standards and add specificity that renders the competency statements measurable.

Results are learning targets we want students to achieve. There are three essential targets that should be evident in the school counseling curriculum: acquisition of relevant knowledge, development of skills that are appropriate to students' educational and career interests, and attitudes/behaviors/value we want students to embrace because they lead to success.

The successful implementation of a school counseling program is opportunity rich. Three essential types of opportunities that must be thoroughly integrated in the school counseling program are the opportunity to learn what we are teaching students, the opportunity to apply what they are learning in authentic contexts and the opportunity for students to demonstrate what they know and can do as a result of participating in the counseling program.

The school counseling curriculum also gives us a way to uniformly assess the progress students are making toward the competency and standard statements. In terms of the curriculum, this means that each activity contains embedded assessments that can help school counselors determine student progress toward, and achievement of, the expected outcomes for each activity. Embedded assessments also contribute to counselors' ability to determine when a student has achieved the student standards defined for the program.

Program Implementation: Planning, Delivery and Evaluation

Planning is a critical process in implementing a CBA. By producing four types of plans (strategic, implementation, counselor-supervisor, personal) it is possible to effectively manage the implementation process through goal setting, action planning and self-reflective activities.

It is important in the delivery of a CBA that data be generated, analyzed and acted upon. Data regarding student progress and achievement must be gathered, organized, analyzed and reported. Data from embedded assessments in the curriculum are a part of this process. But other types of data also play an important role in making these determinations. For example, data from end-of-level assessments can help determine whether students are achieving at expected rates as they transition from elementary to middle to high school and into the post-secondary world. Correlations can be established between student performance in the school counseling program and academic and demographic data. School counseling data must be gathered and reported in a systematic fashion so that data can be used to determine need, develop appropriate interventions and evaluate the impact of implementing the school counseling program. Well-organized data can contribute to the efforts of other district-wide programs designed to assist students, such as Response to Intervention (RTI).

A construct-based report card was recommended in Chapter 6 that provides an effective vehicle for communicating student competencies to those who need the information to make informed decisions about how to meet students' needs: counselors, teachers, other professional support staff, parents and administrators. Such a report card is a continuous reporting of student progress from which interventions can be developed and implemented throughout the school year and which can provide valuable information for improving counselor practice. The report card also contributes to the identification and resolution of problem areas for students, both individually and collectively, that must be addressed to help build capacity for success.

In addition to generating and reporting data on individual students, data also play a crucial role in promoting the value and substantive contribution of the school counseling program to others. It has been our experience that there is a significant lack of understanding about what school counselors do outside of the counseling department, often times within the school itself. Collaboration with other members of the school community with shared data-gathering responsibilities can go a long way toward resolving this problem. In addition, the use of school counselor accountability report cards, discussed in Chapter 6, is a good example of how the contributions of school counselors to student achievement and success can be effectively communicated to others.

CBA's Contribution to Other Initiatives

This is an age of school improvement initiatives. The school counseling profession, like other educational professions, is striving to redefine its knowledge and skill requirements to more clearly define what students should be expected to learn and demonstrate. Reform initiatives are paying attention to the integral relationships among student standards, effective instruction and student assessment.

A CBA proposed a new set of standards and competencies grounded in research that shows them to be important to student success and within the realm of the school counselor. In terms of instruction, a core school counseling curriculum is delivered to all students. Curriculum activities contain embedded assessments to provide immediate feedback to students regarding their performance. The CBA provides other student assessments that can be used to look at student progress at the end of a level. Most importantly, from the perspective of student assessment, the assessment results are issued with report cards so there are multiple opportunities to examine each student's status.

The CBA can contribute to other initiatives in significant ways, particularly to intervention initiatives such as RTI, PBIS and EWS. These initiatives have common goals and skills sets that are also addressed in the CBA.

Alignment with Government Policies and Regulations

Districts are required by state and federal regulations to provide high-quality educational opportunities delivered by highly qualified educators. It is important for school counselors to be able to demonstrate how the counseling program is contributing to the district meeting these mandates. It is through such a process that school counselors can be seen as effective change agents and significant contributors to student achievement and well-being.

How to Begin

How do we begin to transform school counseling into a construct-based program? Three key areas must be addressed: a) defining excellence, b) delivering curriculum and c) assessing students. Student excellence needs to be defined in terms of construct-based, context-sensitive standards and competencies that are supported by research.

Potential standard and competency statements have been proposed in this book. The standard statements serve as the end-of-program (by graduation) learning targets we want students to achieve. The competency statements are aligned with the standards and help build student proficiency by providing specific learning targets along the K–12 learning continuum.

Assessing student progress toward standards and competencies is essential to the transformation process for it helps establish where they are in relation to where we expect them to be along the learning continuum. Assessment data can be immediately used to determine where expectations are being met and where changes and additional support are needed.

SCHOOL COUNSELOR ACCOUNTABILITY

Accountability is what we are responsible for accomplishing as school counselors. In terms of school counseling student standards, we are accountable for helping students achieve the proficiency-building competencies and end-of-program standards we have established for them. We are accountable for providing students with optimal learning opportunities that help them envision their future selves and prepare for maximizing their potential in school and in the post-secondary world.

What does true accountability mean? It means that we are acutely aware of what is involved in student development and how we, as school counselors, can help students become highly motivated, self-directed learners who are knowledgeable about themselves, engaged in meaningful relationships and contributors to the well-being of our world.

True accountability means that we wake up each morning with a compelling desire to serve students and their families, and work collaboratively with our colleagues to help ensure students' success in school, work and life. True accountability means that we continuously ask what difference we can and are making in our students' lives. And to help keep the importance of the difference we make in perspective, we must also consider what opportunities and potential would be lost to our students and our world if we were not there to guide them along their way.

References

ACT. (2011). *Enhancing college and career readiness and success: The role of academic behaviors.* Iowa City, IA: Author.

ACT. (2012). *The condition of college and career readiness, 2012.* Iowa City, IA: Author.

Alvarez, J. A., & Emory, E. (2006). Executive function and the frontal lobes: A meta-analytic review. *Neuropsychology Review, 16*(1), 17–42.

Ambrose, S. A., Bridges, M. W., DiPietro, M., Lovett, M. C., & Norman, M. K. (2010). *How learning works: Seven research-based principles for smart teaching.* San Francisco, CA: Jossey-Bass.

American School Counselor Association (ASCA). (2012). *The ASCA national model: A framework for school counseling programs* (3rd ed.). Alexandria, VA: Author.

Anderman, E. M., Anderman, L. H., & Griesinger, T. (1999). The relationship of present and possible academic selves during early adolescence to grade point average and achievement goals. *The Elementary School Journal, 100,* 3–17.

APA. (1997). *Learner-centered psychological principles: A framework for school reform and redesign.* Washington, DC: Author.

Atkinson, J. W., & Feather, N. T. (Eds.). (1966). *A theory of achievement motivation.* New York, NY: Wiley.

Bandura, A. (1997). *Self-efficacy: The exercise of control.* New York, NY: Worth Publishers.

Batsche, G., Elliott, J., Graden, J. L., Grimes, J., Kovaleski, J. F., Prasse, D. et al. (2005). *Response to Intervention: Policy considerations and implementation.* Alexandria, VA: National Association of State Directors of Special Education. Retrieved from http://www.pbis.org/pbis_newsletter/volume_4/issue2.aspx

Beale, U. (2004). Family is someone to tuck you into bed: Teaching a unit on family diversity. In M. Shamnsher, E. Decker, G. Brandes, & D. Kelly (Eds.), *Teaching for social justice.* Vancouver, BC: British Columbia Teachers' Federation.

Beelmann, A., Pfingsten, U., & Losel, F. (1994). Effects of training social competence in children: A meta-analysis of recent evaluation studies. *Journal of Clinical Child Psychology, 23,* 260–271.

Bell, L. (1997). Theoretical foundations for social justice education. In M. Adams, L. Bell, & P. Griffin (Eds.), *Teaching for diversity and social justice.* New York, NY: Routledge.

Blair, C. (2002). School readiness: Integrating cognition and emotion in a neurobiological conceptualization of children's functioning at school entry. *American Psychologist, 57,* 111–127.

Blair, C., & Diamond, A. (2008). Biological processes in prevention and intervention: The promotion of self-regulation as a means of preventing school failure. *Development and Psychopathology, 20,* 899–911.

Blair, C., & Razza, R. P. (2007). Relating effortful control, executive function, and false belief understanding to emerging math and literacy ability in kindergarten. *Child Development, 78,* 647–663.

Brodie, I. (2012, June 12). The top 10 ways school counselors can support teachers. *Homeroom: The Official Blog of the U.S. Department of Education.* Retrieved July 8, 2013, from http://www.ed.gov/blog/2012/06/the-top-10-ways-school-counselors-can-support-teachers/

Bronson, G., Gurney, J. G., Land, G. H. (1999). Evidence-based decisions making in public health. *Journal of Public Health Management, 5,* 86–97.

Brooks, J. G., & Thompson, E. G. (2005). Social justice in the classroom. *Educational Leadership, 63,* 48–52.

Brown, T. E. (2006). Executive functions and attention deficit hyperactivity sisorder: Implications of two conflicting views. *International Journal of Disability, Development and Education, 53,* 35–46.

Bruce, M., Bridgeland, J. M., Fox, J. H., & Balfanz, R. (2011). *On track for success: The use of early warning indicator and systems to build a grad nation.* Washington, DC: Civic Enterprises.

Campbell, C. A., & Dahir, C. A. (1997). *Sharing the vision: The national standards for school counseling programs.* Alexandria, VA: American School Counselor Association Press.

Carey, J. C., Brigman, G., Webb, L., Villares, E., & Harrington, K. (in press). Development of an instrument to measure student use of academic success skills: An exploratory factor analysis. *Measurement and Evaluation in Counseling and Development.*

Carey, J. C., & Dimmitt, C. (2012). School counseling and student outcomes: Summary of six statewide studies. *Professional School Counseling, 16*(2), 146–153.

Carey, J. C., Harrington, K., Hoffman, D., & Martin, I. (2012). A statewide evaluation of the outcomes of ASCA National Model school counseling programs in rural and suburban Nebraska high schools. *Professional School Counseling, 16,* 100–107.

Carey, J. C., Harrington, K., Martin, I., & Stevens, D. (2012). A statewide evaluation of the outcomes of the implementation of ASCA National Model school counseling programs in high schools in Utah. *Professional School Counseling, 16,* 89–99.

Casey, B. J., Jones, R. M., & Hare, T. A. (2008). The adolescent brain. *Annals of the New York Academy of Science, 1124,* 111–126.

Chwalisz, K. (2003). Evidence-based practice: A framework for twenty-first-century scientist-practitioner training. *Counseling Psychologist, 31,* 497–528.

Clark, C. A. C., Pritchard, V. E., & Woodward, L. J. (2010). Preschool executive functioning abilities predict early mathematics achievement. *Developmental Psychology, 46,* 1176–1191.

Cognition. (n.d.). In *Wikipedia, The Free Encyclopedia.* Retrieved March 27, 2014, from http://en.wikipedia.org/wiki/Cognition

Cokley, K. O., Bernard, N., Cunningham, D., & Motoike, J. (2001). A psychometric investigation of the academic motivation scale using a United States sample. *Measurement and Evaluation in Counseling and Development, 34,* 109–119.

College Board, National Office for School Counselor Advocacy (NOSCA). (2010). *Eight components of college and career readiness counseling*. Washington, DC: Author.

Conley, David T. (2013, January 22). Rethinking the notion of "noncognitive." *Education Week*. Retrieved November 27, 2013, from http://www.edweek.org/ew/articles/2013/01/23/18conley.h32.html?r=734759030&tkn=OMYFtvGvk3 G6OI%2FKuI9WA6jey6HFUNLyQE1g&print=1

Corno, L. (1992). Encouraging students to take responsibility for learning and performance. *Elementary School Journal, 93,* 69–83.

Darling-Hammond, L., French, J., & Garcia-Lopez, S. (Eds.). (2002). *Learning to teach for social justice*. New York, NY: Teachers College Press.

Day, J. D., Borkowski, J. G., Punzo, D., & Howsepian, D. (1994). Enhancing possible selves in Mexican American children. *Motivation and Emotion, 18,* 79–103.

Deaton, C. (2001). Outcomes measurement and evidence-based nursing practice. *Journal of Cardiovascular Nursing, 15,* 83–86.

Deci, E. L., Eghrari, H., Patrick, B. C., & Leone, D. R. (1994). Facilitating internalization: The self-determination theory perspective. *Journal of Personality, 62,* 119–142.

Denham S. A., Ji, P., & Hamre, B. (2010). Compendium of preschool through elementary school social-emotional learning and associated assessment measures. Chicago, IL: CASEL. http://casel.org/wp-content/uploads/Compendium_SELTools.pdf

Diamond, A., & Lee, K. (2011). Interventions shown to aid executive function development in children 4 to 12 years old. *Science, 333,* 959–964.

Dimmitt, C., Carey, J. C., & Hatch, T. A. (2007). *Evidence-based school counseling: Making a difference with data-driven practices*. New York, NY: Corwin.

Durlak, J. A., Weissberg, R. P., Dymnicki, A. B., Taylor, R. D., & Schellinger, K. B. (2011). The impact of enhancing students' social and emotional learning: A meta-analysis of school-based universal interventions. *Child Development, 82,* 405–432.

DuPaul, G. J., & Stoner, G. (2003). *ADHD in schools: Assessment and intervention strategies*. New York, NY: Guilford.

Elliot, R. (2003). Executive functions and their disorders. *British Medical Bulletin, 65,* 49–59.

Flavell, J. H. (1987). Speculations about the nature and development of metacognition. In F. Weinert & R. Kluwe (Eds.), *Metacognition, motivation, and understanding* (pp. 21–29). Hillsdale, NJ: Erlbaum.

Fraser, M. W., Galinsky, M. J., Smokowski, P. R., Day, S. H., Terzian, M. A., Rose, R. A., & Guo, S. (2005). Social information-processing skills training to promote social competence and prevent aggressive behavior in third grade. *Journal of Consulting and Clinical Psychology, 73*(6), 1045–1055.

Gibbs, J., Potter, G., & Goldstein, A. (1995). *The EQUIP program: Teaching youth to think and act responsibility through a peer-helping approach*. Champaign, IL: Research Press.

Graziano, P. A., Reavis, R. D., Keane, S. P., & Calkins, S. D. (2007). The role of emotion regulation in children's early academic success. *Journal of School Psychology, 45,* 3–19.

Gumora, G., & Arsenio, W. F. (2002). Emotionality, emotion regulation, and school performance in middle school children. *Journal of School Psychology, 40,* 395–413.

Hacker, D. J., Dunlosky, J., & Graesser, A. C. (Eds.). (2009). *Handbook of metacognition in education.* Mahwah, NJ: Erlbaum/Taylor & Francis.

Hawaii Department of Education. (2013). Standards-based report cards. http://reportcard.k12.hi.us

Heckman, J. J., & Krueger, A. B. (2003). *Inequality in America: What role for human capital policies?* Cambridge, MA: MIT Press.

Honig, A. S., & Wittmer, D. S. (1996). Helping children become more prosocial: Ideas for classrooms, families, schools, and communities. *Young Children, 51,* 62–70.

Johnson, S., & Johnson, C. D. (2003). Results-based guidance: A systems approach to student support programs. *ASCA Professional School Counseling, 6,* 180–184.

Johnson, S., Johnson, C. D., & Downs, L. (2006). *Building a results-based student support program.* Boston, MA: Lahaska Press, Houghton Mifflin Company.

Joint Committee on Standards for Educational Evaluation. (2003). *The student evaluation standards: How to improve evaluations of students.* Newbury Park, CA: Corwin.

Jones, E. E., & Berglas, S. (1978). Control of attributions about the self through self-handicapping strategies: The appeal of alcohol and the role of underachievement. *Personality and Social Psychology Bulletin, 4,* 200–206.

Kincheloe, J., & Steinberg, S. (1993). A tentative description of post-formal thinking: The critical confrontation with cognitive theory. *Harvard Educational Review, 63,* 296–320.

Kratochwill, T. T., & Shernoff, E. S. (2003). Evidence-based practice: Promoting evidence-based interventions. *School Psychology Quarterly, 18,* 389–408.

Lalas, J. (2007). Teaching for social justice in multicultural urban schools: Conceptualization and classroom implication. *Multicultural Education, 4,* 17–21.

Leondari, A., Syngollitou, E., & Kiosseoglou, G. (1998). Academic achievement, motivation and possible selves. *Journal of Adolescence, 21,* 219–222.

Levin, H. M. (2012). More than just test scores. *PROSPECTS: UNESCO's Quarterly Review of Comparative Education.* http://link.springer.com/journal/11125

Locke, E. A. (1996). Motivation through conscious goal setting. *Applied and Preventive Psychology, 5,* 117–124.

Locke, E. A. (2001). Motivation by goal setting. *Handbook of Organizational Behavior, 2,* 43–54.

Lucas, T. (2005). Fostering a commitment to social justice through service learning in a teacher education course. In N. Michelli & D. Keiser (Eds.), *Teacher education for democracy and social justice.* New York and London: Routledge.

Mardziah, H. (2001). *Self-directed learning.* Bloomington, IL: ERIC Digest.

Markus, H., & Nurius, P. (1986). Possible selves. *American Psychologist, 41,* 954–969.

Maynus, L. (n.d.). *Understanding depth of knowledge.* Retrieved November 29, 2013, from http://sh.educonv.com/presentations/72571/index.html

McClelland, D. C. (1965). Toward a theory of motive acquisition. *American Psychologist, 20,* 321–333.

McCraty, R., Atkinson, M., Tomasino, D., Goelitz, J., & Mayrovitz, H. N. (1999). The impact of an emotional self-management skills course on psychosocial functioning and autonomic recovery to stress in middle school children. *Integrative Physiology and Behavioral Science, 34*(4), 246–268.

McGinnis, E., & Goldstein, A. (1997). *Skillstreaming the elementary school child: New strategies and perspectives for teaching prosocial skills.* Champaign, IL: Research Press.

McLaughlin, M. & Devoogd, G. (2004). Critical literacy as comprehension: Expanding reader response. *The Reading Teacher, 48,* 52–62.

Merrell, K. W. (1993). *School Social Behavior Scales.* Iowa City, IA: Assessment-Intervention Resources.

Morisano, D., Hirsh, J. B., Peterson, J. B., Pihl, R. O., & Shore, B. M. (2010). Setting, elaborating, and reflecting on personal goals improves academic performance. *Journal of Applied Psychology, 95,* 255–264.

Moss, C. M., Brookhart, S. M., & Long, B. A. (2011). Knowing your learning target. *Educational Leadership, 68*(6), 66–69.

National Governors Association Center for Best Practices, Council of Chief State School Officers. (2010). *Common Core State Standards.* Washington, DC: Author.

Nelson-Le Gall, S. (1981). Help-seeking: An understudied problem-solving skill in children. *Developmental Review, 1,* 224–246.

Nelson-Le Gall, S. (1985). Help-seeking behavior in learning. In E. W. Gordon (Ed.), *Review of research in education* (Vol. 12, pp. 55–90). Washington, DC: American Educational Research Association.

Newman, R. S. (1994). Adaptive help-seeking: A strategy of self-regulated learning. In D. Schunk & B. Zimmerman (Eds.), *Self-regulation of learning and performance: Issues and educational applications* (pp. 283–301). Hillsdale, NJ: Erlbaum.

Oyserman, D., Bybee, D., & Terry, K. (2006). Possible selves and academic outcomes: How and when possible selves impel action. *Journal of Personality and Social Psychology, 91,* 188–204.

Oyserman, D., Gant, L., & Anger, J. (1995). A socially contextualized model of African American identity: Possible selves school persistence. *Journal of Personality and Social Psychology, 69,* 1216–1232.

Oyserman, D., & Markus, H. R. (1990). Possible selves and delinquency. *Journal of Personality and Social Psychology, 59,* 112–125.

Partnership for 21st Century Skills (2011). *P21 Common core toolkit.* Washington, DC: Author.

Payton, J. W., Weissberg, R. P., Durlak, J. A., Dymnicki, A. B., Taylor, R. D., Schellinger, K. B., & Pachan, M. (2008). *The positive impact of social and emotional learning for kindergarten to eighth-grade students: Findings from three scientific reviews* (Technical Report). Chicago, IL: Collaborative for Academic, Social, and Emotional Learning.

PBIS.org. (n.d.). Response to Intervention (RTI) & PBIS. Retrieved November 30, 2013, from http://www.pbis.org/school/rti.aspx

Pintrich, P. R., & DeGroot, E. V. (1990). Motivational and self-regulated learning components of classroom academic performance. *Journal of Educational Psychology, 82,* 33–40.

Pintrich, P. R., & Schunk, D. (2002). *Motivation in education: Theory, research, and applications* (2nd ed.). Upper Saddle. NJ: Prentice-Hall.

Poynton, T. A., & Carey, J. C. (2006). An integrated model of data-based decision making for school counseling. *Professional School Counseling, 10,* 121–130.

Rapee, R. M., Schniering, C. A., & Hudson, J. L. (2009). Anxiety disorders during childhood and adolescence: Origins and treatment. *Annual Review Clinical Psychology, 5,* 311–341.

Reid, R., Trout, A. L., & Schartz, M. (2005). Self-regulation interventions for children with attention deficit/hyperactivity disorder. *Council for Exceptional Children, 71*(4), 361–377.

Robbins, S., Lauver, K., Le, H., Davis, D., Langley, R., & Carlstrom, A. (2004). Do psychosocial and study skill factors predict college outcomes? A meta-analysis. *Psychological Bulletin, 130,* 261–288.

Rotter, J. B. (1990). Internal versus external control of reinforcement: A case history of a variable. *American Psychologist, 45,* 489–493.

Ryan, R. M., & Deci, E. L. (2000). Self-determination theory and the facilitation of intrinsic motivation, social development, and well-being. *American Psychologist, 55,* 68–78.

Sackett, D. L., Straus, S. E., Richardson, W. S., Rosenberg, W., & Hayes, R. B. (2000). *Evidence-based medicine: How to practice and teach EBM* (2nd ed.). Edinburgh, Scotland, UK: Churchill Livingstone.

Schraw, G. (1998). Promoting general metacognitive awareness. *Instructional Science, 26,* 113–125.

Secretary's Commission on Achieving Necessary Skills. (1991). *What work requires of schools: A SCANS report for America 2000.* Washington, DC: U.S. Department of Labor.

Semple, R. J., Lee, J., Rosa, D. & Miller, L. F. (2010). A randomized trial of mindfulness-based cognitive therapy for children: Promoting mindful attention to enhance social-emotional resiliency in children. *Journal of Child and Family Studies, 19*(2), 218–229.

Sexton, T. L., Schofield, T. L., & Whiston, S. C. (1997). Evidence-based practice: A pragmatic model to unify counseling. *Counseling and Human Development, 4,* 1–18.

Seligman, M. (2006). *Learned optimism: How to change your mind and your life.* New York, NY: Random House.

Seligman, M., & Nolen-Hoeksema, S. (1987). Explanatory style and depression. In D. Magnusson and A. Ohman. *Psychopathology: An Interactional Perspective* (pp. 125–139). New York: Academic Press.

Shields, A., & Cicchetti, D. (1997). Emotion regulation among school-age children: The development and validation of a new criterion Q-sort scale. *Developmental Psychology, 33,* 906–917.

Shields, A., Dickstein, S., Seifer, R., Guisti, L., Magee, K. D., & Spritz, B. (2001). Emotional competence and early school adjustment: A study of preschoolers at risk. *Early Education and Development, 12,* 73–96.

Trilling, B., & Fadel, C. (2009). *21st century skills: Learning for life in our times.* San Francisco, CA: Jossey-Bass.

U.S. Department of Education. (2013, March 10). No Child Left Behind. Standards and Assessments: Non-regulatory guidance. Retrieved from https://www2.ed.gov/policy/elsec/guid/saaguidance03.doc

U.S. Department of Health and Human Services Office of Population Affairs. (2013). *Maturation of the Prefrontal Cortex.* http://www.hhs.gov/opa/familylife/tech_assistance/etraining/adolescent_brain/Development/prefrontal_cortex/

U.S. Office of Special Education Programs (OSEP). (2009, May 24). Technical Assistance Center on School-Wide Positive Behavioral Interventions and Supports. Retrieved from http://www.pbis.org/about_us/default.aspx

Vallerand, R. J., Pelletier, L. G., Blais, M. R, Brière, N. M., Senécal, C., & Vallières, E. F. (1992). The academic motivation scale: A measure of intrinsic, extrinsic, and amotivation in education. *Educational and Psychological Measurement, 52,* 1003–1017.

Walker, H. M. (1983). *The ACCESS program: Adolescent curriculum for communication and effective social skills: Student study guide.* Austin, TX: Pro-Ed.

Webb, N. (2005). *Alignment: Powerful tool for focusing instruction, curricula, and assessment.* Presented at TILSA Alignment Tool Dissemination Workshop, July 25–26, 2005, Boston, MA. Retrieved November 20, 2013, from http://view .officeapps.live.com/op/view.aspx?src=http%3A%2F%2Fwat.wceruw.org%2F TILSA%2520Dissemination%2520Webb%2520presentation%2520for%2520T raining%2520%2520July%252024%2520%25202005.ppt

Webb, N. L., Alt, M., Ely, R., & Vesperman, B. (2005). *Web Alignment Tool (WAT) training manual.* Madison, WI: Wisconsin Center for Educational Research.

Webb, L. D., Brigman, G. A., & Campbell, C. (2005). Linking school counselors and student success: A replication of the Student Success Skills approach targeting the academic and social competence of students. *Professional School Counseling, 8*(5), 407–411.

Wiener, B. (1974). *Achievement motivation and attribution theory.* Morristown, NJ: General Learning Press.

Willcutt, E. G., Doyle, A. E., Nigg, J. T., Faraone, S. V., & Pennington, B. F. (2005). Validity of the Executive Function theory of attention-deficit/hyperactivity disorder: A meta-analytic review. *Biological Psychiatry, 57,* 1336–1346.

Willoughby, M. T, Wirth, R. J., Blair, C. B., Greenberg, M., & The Family Life Project Investigators. (2012). The measurement of executive function at age 5: Psychometric properties and relationship to academic achievement. *Psychological Assessment, 24,* 226–239.

Zeman, J., Shipman, K., & Penza-Clyve, S. (2001). Development and initial validation of the Children's Sadness Management Scale. *Journal of Nonverbal Behavior, 25,* 187–205.

Zimmerman, B. J. (1990). Self-regulated learning and academic achievement: An overview. *Educational Psychologist, 25,* 3-17.1

Zimmerman, B. J., & Martinez-Pons, M. (1988). Construct validation of a strategy model of student self-regulated learning. *Journal of Educational Psychology, 80,* 284–290.

Zins, J., Weissbert, R., Wang, M., & Walberg, H. (2004). *Building academic success on social and emotional learning: What does the research say?* New York, NY: Teachers College Press.

Index